THE
VIETNAM
WAR

THE
VIETNAM WAR

A CONCISE INTERNATIONAL HISTORY

MARK ATWOOD LAWRENCE

OXFORD
UNIVERSITY PRESS

2008

OXFORD
UNIVERSITY PRESS

Oxford University Press, Inc., publishes works that further
Oxford University's objective of excellence
in research, scholarship, and education.

Oxford   New York
Auckland   Cape Town   Dar es Salaam   Hong Kong   Karachi
Kuala Lumpur   Madrid   Melbourne   Mexico City   Nairobi
New Delhi   Shanghai   Taipei   Toronto

With offices in
Argentina   Austria   Brazil   Chile   Czech Republic   France   Greece
Guatemala   Hungary   Italy   Japan   Poland   Portugal   Singapore
South Korea   Switzerland   Thailand   Turkey   Ukraine   Vietnam

ISBN 978-0-19-531465-6

Printed in the United States of America

ACKNOWLEDGMENTS

It is my great pleasure to acknowledge the assistance I received from numerous institutions and individuals in writing this book. I am grateful above all to the two universities that jointly enabled me to complete the project under ideal conditions. At Yale University, I owe an enormous debt to the Department of History, the International Security Studies program, and Mr. and Mrs. Landon T. Clay. At the University of Texas at Austin, I wish to thank the Department of History and the College of Liberal Arts. I am especially indebted to Ted Bromund, John Lewis Gaddis, Paul Kennedy, Ben Kiernan, and John Merriman in New Haven, and to David Oshinsky, Michael Stoff, and Alan Tully in Austin.

I am also grateful to a number of individuals who generously commented on drafts of all or parts of this book. Their suggestions not only tightened my analysis and saved me from errors but also reminded me how fortunate I am to have such supportive and talented friends and colleagues. My sincere thanks go to William J. Duiker, Jeffrey Engel, Fredrik Logevall, Edward Miller, Lien-Hang T. Nguyen, Steph Osbakken, Jon Persoff, Andrew Preston, Paul Rubinson, and Bradley Woodworth. Most of all, I am indebted to Christopher Goscha, who meticulously critiqued the entire manuscript and generously shared his extraordinary expertise on the Vietnamese side of the war. Thanks also to

Charles Keith and Helen Pho, who helped track down elusive information. At Oxford University Press, Susan Ferber marked up every page with her trademark thoroughness and shepherded the project to completion with a perfect blend of patience and enthusiasm. Christine Dahlin helped immeasurably with the final stages.

I also wish to acknowledge the monumental intellectual debts I owe to those historians who have led the way for many years in writing about the Vietnam War. If this book has merit, it is partly due to that fact that it stands, as Sir Isaac Newton might have put it, on the shoulders of giants such as David L. Anderson, William J. Duiker, David W. P. Elliott, Lloyd C. Gardner, George C. Herring, David G. Marr, Robert J. McMahon, Robert D. Schulzinger, and Marilyn B. Young. I am humbled by their accomplishments and grateful for their inspiring examples. The book also stands on the shoulders of those who have helped me in more personal ways. For their support in this and so many other endeavors, my deepest thanks go to Steph Osbakken; to Jane, Elizabeth, Priscilla, and Patrick Melampy; and to Robert and Elizabeth Atwood Lawrence.

CONTENTS

THE
VIETNAM
WAR

INTRODUCTION

AMERICANS AND OTHER WESTERNERS CALL IT SIMPLY "the Vietnam War," but the fighting that took place in Vietnam between 1961 and 1975 has many names. The Vietnamese call it the "American War" to distinguish it from confrontations with other foreign enemies during their country's bloody twentieth century. Scholars and others striving for greater detachment prefer the "Second Indochina War" to mark it off from earlier and later conflicts and to emphasize that the fighting engulfed not just Vietnam but Cambodia and Laos as well. During the war, still other names prevailed. The Vietnamese communists labeled it grandly the "War of Liberation" or the "Anti-U.S. War of National Salvation." American leaders, eager to downplay its significance, often called it merely the "Vietnam conflict."[1]

War or conflict? *The* Vietnam war or just one of many? War of liberation or something less heroic? Merely an episode in Vietnamese history or part of regional, perhaps even global, processes? It depends, of course, on one's point of view. Since journalists, memoirists, historians, and other commentators started writing about the war in the 1960s, the overwhelming majority of books and articles have examined it from the standpoint of the United States. They have, that is, relied on American sources and analyzed the war as an episode in American history. This tendency is hardly surprising. Of the major participants in the war, the United States has gone furthest in allowing researchers access to once-secret documentation. It is therefore simply more feasible to write authoritatively about U.S. behavior than that of other countries. Moreover, by far the most intense controversies have swirled around the American role in the war. It has therefore seemed especially urgent to understand why Americans acted as they did.

Only in recent years have the outlooks and experiences of the other belligerents received detailed attention. In part, this trend grows from a mounting desire among scholars to move beyond old polemical battles and to understand the war in all its complexity. More than anything, though, it reflects the availability of new source material since the collapse of the Soviet bloc in the late 1980s and early 1990s and the opening of Vietnam to the outside world during the same period. Before these developments, documentary records reflecting North Vietnamese, South Vietnamese, Chinese, Soviet, and East European calculations were off-limits to historians, kept secret by authoritarian governments with no desire to open their national security decisions to scrutiny. The end of the Cold War altered the situation by decreasing sensitivities in many countries about recent history. For the first time, scholars gained access, albeit incomplete and sometimes temporary, to archival collections that enabled them to penetrate old walls of secrecy.

The resulting wave of scholarship has revolutionized the study of the Vietnam War—the term this book will employ because of its familiarity to Western readers—in various ways. Most simply, new research has begun exposing the motives and calculations that drove policymakers in Hanoi and Saigon as well as in Beijing, Moscow, and other capitals around the world. At the same time, scholars working with Vietnamese sources have gone further than ever before toward understanding the attitudes of ordinary Vietnamese who fought on both sides of the conflict. On a more conceptual level, sources from around the world have enabled historians to view the war more fully than before as an episode in global history—an expression of phenomena such as decolonization and the rise of international communism. The new scholarship has also brought new subtlety to the study of the American role in the war. Documentation from other countries has revealed the considerable extent to which decisions made elsewhere shaped, constrained, and sometimes determined U.S. choices. Moreover, the new studies have informed the debates that continue to preoccupy Americans. Was the war winnable in any meaningful sense? Was there ever a realistic chance for a negotiated settlement? Was the Vietnamese revolution fundamentally communist or nationalist in character? Deep knowledge of Vietnamese, Chinese, and Soviet behavior is essential to answer these questions persuasively.

This book aims to take account of this new scholarship in a brief, accessible narrative of the Vietnam War. It is, as the subtitle suggests, an international history. More specifically, it places the war within the long flow of Vietnamese history and then captures the goals and experiences of various governments that became deeply embroiled in the country during the second half of the twentieth century. The book does not, however, displace the United States from the center of the story. In fact, it examines the American side of the war in considerable detail. Emphasis on the U.S. role makes sense given the significance of the controversies centering on American decision making—controversies that, if anything, only grew more intense in the early twenty-first century as the U.S. embroilment in the Middle East stoked new debate about the lessons of the Vietnam War. Careful examination of the U.S. role is also appropriate given the remarkable richness of recent scholarship on American behavior. While internationally minded historians have exploited archives in Hanoi, Moscow, and elsewhere, American historians have achieved unprecedented depth in their explorations of U.S. policymaking, politics, public opinion, and the experiences of U.S. soldiers.

The goal of this book, then, is to strike a balance by examining the American role within a broadly international context. To make the task manageable and to ensure thematic coherence, the following pages focus on answering four questions that have attracted intense scholarly and popular debate. The aim is not so much to answer these questions explicitly and exhaustively as to embed answers within an engaging narrative. But each question deserves brief introduction here.

First, what were the basic motives of the Vietnamese who fought against the United States? This problem has proved enormously difficult for historians, just as it was for U.S. policymakers during the war. Unquestionably, many Vietnamese leaders were dedicated communists who hoped that victory over South Vietnam and the United States would serve the larger interests of international communism. Yet the communists clearly drew a great deal of strength from their ability to harness and manipulate nationalist sentiment that stretched far back into Vietnamese history. French imperial domination in the late nineteenth and early twentieth centuries played an especially crucial role in fueling anticolonial ambitions that helped sustain the communist cause in later years. To elucidate the complex intertwining of communism and nationalism, this book devotes considerable attention to the evolution of Vietnamese revolutionary politics in the decades leading up to the American war. It then attempts to explore the complicated and shifting array of motives that kept Vietnamese revolutionaries fighting for so many years.

Second, why did Vietnam become a focus of dispute among the world's mightiest nations following the Second World War and then remain a major point of conflict for the next half century? Why, in short, did powerful nations invest so much in such a small and impoverished country? Before 1949 or so, governments around the world viewed political turmoil in Vietnam as a matter of minor significance. But the coming of the Cold War changed everything. As the globe split into rival blocs headed by Washington and Moscow, conflict in Vietnam increasingly appeared to be connected to the worldwide struggle between democratic capitalism and international communism. American, Soviet, and Chinese policymakers came to see Vietnam, a resource-rich nation occupying a vital geographic position, as crucial to their chances of prevailing in the global struggle. Vietnam's economic and geostrategic importance does not, however, fully explain the behavior of the great powers. It is also essential to explore how internal political rivalries and pressures—operating within the U.S., Soviet, and Chinese governments as well as within each of the Cold War alliances—drove the major nations to escalate their involvement in Vietnam. The aim here is to capture all of these factors.

Third, why did the Vietnam War turn out the way it did? From the outset of the struggle against French colonialism, Vietnamese revolutionaries faced enemies possessing vast technological and material superiority. And yet they were able to persevere and ultimately prevail over France and, later, the United States. Explaining the U.S. defeat has generated perhaps the single bitterest controversy surrounding the Vietnam War. Some commentators blame weakness and irresolution on the American home front, embodied variously in the antiwar movement, the media, or liberal politicians, for sapping the nation's will and thereby preventing the U.S. military from making the all-out effort that would have brought victory. Others blame American military commanders for pursuing flawed strategies in fighting the war. Still others blame civilian leaders—and, in some formulations, the larger American culture from which they came—for failing to recognize the impossibility of establishing a stable, Western-oriented Vietnamese state that would genuinely command the support of its people. The war was, in this view, unwinnable no matter what methods Americans used to fight it because the United States never won Vietnamese "hearts and minds." This book emphasizes the last explanation but also suggests that examination of U.S. policymaking does not yield all the answers. The Vietnamese communists prevailed in part because of their own political and military strategies and their success in obtaining material assistance from abroad.

Fourth, what are the legacies of the Vietnam War? The book's final chapter attempts to answer this question with reference to both Southeast Asia and the United States. In Vietnam, Cambodia, and Laos, the war left intense political rivalries that fueled a new round of internal and international conflict during the late 1970s and throughout the 1980s. Over the longer term, the war left a trail of bitterness, suffering, and environmental devastation that continued to reverberate in the twenty-first century. Many thousands of Americans struggled with the physical impact of war, but, for the United States as a whole, the most enduring legacy was psychological. Defeat bitterly divided Americans according to the lessons they drew from it. Some viewed the lost war as evidence of fundamental national failings and urged a thorough reappraisal of the way the government made decisions and wielded power abroad. Others drew the opposite conclusion, arguing that the United States must proceed with greater boldness and certainty to avoid similar setbacks in the future.

No book—certainly not such a slim one as this—can do full justice to all of these themes. Yet this introductory study can play a vital role in bridging the gap that too often separates scholars, with their deep knowledge of small slices of the past, from general readers interested in understanding the broad flow of history. If the book brings greater awareness to ongoing debates over the Vietnam War, its mission will be accomplished. If it sparks interest in further reading about the war and its meaning, so much the better.

THE ROAD TO REVOLUTION

"HOW DID THE AGONY BEGIN?" A *NEW YORK TIMES*
reporter posed the question on July 6, 1971, a few weeks after the
paper began publishing excerpts of a U.S. government study on
the origins of the war raging in Vietnam.[1] The top-secret report,
leaked by a disgruntled Defense Department aide, promised answers. But not even seven thousand pages of analysis offered
clarity. Indeed, decades of subsequent scholarly inquiry have
failed to resolve many uncertainties and controversies surrounding the war's origins.

Among the conundrums is a deceptively simple question: How
far back into the past do the roots of the Vietnam War extend?
When, in other words, should a history of the war begin? Some
commentators locate the causes of the war in relatively recent
times—in the 1940s, for example, when conflict in Vietnam became enmeshed in the Cold War, or in the early 1960s, when the
United States dramatically expanded its military role in the
country. Others reach much further back, tracing the origins of
the war to Vietnamese struggles against foreign domination many
decades or even centuries before Americans took interest in
Southeast Asia.

Those who insist on a comparatively recent starting date un-questionably have a point. Contrary to the claims of Vietnamese communists, the war was no simple extension of Vietnam's inde-pendence struggles in earlier eras. Rather, it resulted from specific decisions made in the mid-twentieth century by leaders in Viet-nam, the United States, and other countries. Yet to begin the story of the war in the 1940s or 1960s risks repeating the errors of U.S. policymakers by ignoring the deep roots of the social and political turmoil that made Vietnam an arena of international conflict during the Cold War. Only by examining the long flow of Viet-namese history is it possible to grasp the nature of the revolutionary movement against which the United States went to war in 1965.

IMPERIAL ENCOUNTERS

Powerful outsiders had shaped Vietnamese life for two thousand years by the time American troops arrived in Southeast Asia. The earliest and most persistent foreign power to play this role was China, which conquered the "Viet" ethnic group in 111 B.C. and ruled its territory as a province of the Chinese empire for the next millennium. During that epoch, the Vietnamese developed a complicated relationship with their Chinese overlords. On the one hand, they drew heavily on Chinese culture, adapting the religious practices, technology, art, architecture, music, and language of their northern neighbors to Vietnamese conditions. Perhaps most striking, they embraced China's form of govern-ment, a hierarchical system administered by mandarins steeped in Confucian ethics and philosophy.

On the other hand, Chinese domination spurred Vietnamese elites to launch a series of bloody revolts against the empire—David-versus-Goliath uprisings celebrated in the twentieth cen-tury as manifestations of an allegedly timeless nationalist spirit and resourcefulness in battling mighty enemies. In 39 A.D., Trung Trac and her sister Trung Nhi led the most fabled rebellion of all, vanquishing a superior Chinese force and establishing an independent Viet kingdom. When China quashed the rebellion three years later, the Trung sisters drowned themselves in a river, assuring their status as martyrs for twentieth-century nationalists.

Only the crumbling of China's T'ang dynasty in the tenth century opened the way for lasting Vietnamese independence. As in later periods, Vietnam's political development owed much to a shift in the larger geopolitical environment. Beset by corruption and unrest at home, the Chinese could no longer muster the resources to maintain colonial control. The decisive moment came in 939, when a Vietnamese army destroyed a much larger Chinese force by cleverly ambushing it near modern-day Haiphong. Thereafter, China periodically threatened to restore its rule over Vietnam, and it succeeded in doing so for a brief period in the fifteenth century. For the most part, however, the new state of "Dai Viet" ("Great Viet") kept the Chinese behemoth at bay through skillful diplomacy, tribute payments to the Chinese court, and periodic military campaigns against invading armies.

Independence brought greater stability and prosperity, but it ultimately produced new kinds of conflict that left a deep imprint on modern Vietnam. First the Vietnamese, showing new expansionist desires of their own, vanquished their southern neighbors, the Cham and Khmer kingdoms, in a series of wars starting in the fifteenth century. Previously, the Vietnamese had been confined to the region around the Red River Delta, hemmed in on three sides by mountains and the sea. Population growth and economic ambition led them to covet the fertile coastal plain to their south and the vast Mekong Delta beyond, areas controlled for centuries by the Cham and Khmer peoples. By about 1700,

Vietnam's expansion was complete. The S-shaped country—regarded by its Southeast Asian neighbors as a fearsome imperial power—stretched along eight hundred miles of coast from the Chinese border to the Gulf of Thailand.

As it grew, however, Vietnam fell victim to a new problem: internal dissension. Spread over a much larger area, the Vietnamese lost much of the political and social cohesion that had bound them together. Rulers in Hanoi found it difficult to exert influence over long distances. Meanwhile southerners, benefiting from readily available land and higher crop yields, developed a more entrepreneurial and individualistic ethos than prevailed in the tradition-bound north—a cultural gap that persisted for centuries to come. Combined with antagonisms between Vietnamese princes, these centrifugal forces led in 1613 to a civil war that resulted in the division of Vietnam into two parts headed by rival warrior families, the Nguyen in the south and the Trinh in the north.

Civil strife continued off and on for two hundred years until the leader of the southern family succeeded in imposing precarious unity in the early nineteenth century and established the Nguyen dynasty. The Nguyen emperors named their domain "Nam Viet" ("Southern Viet") and sought to consolidate their state through the invigoration of Confucian practices. Within a few decades, however, they faced a new challenge to the unity and independence of their territories. Starting in the 1860s, France gradually colonized Vietnam and its western neighbors, Cambodia and Laos. As in so much of the world that fell under European domination around the same time, the process transformed the region and set the stage for turmoil in the twentieth century.

European missionaries had been active in Vietnam since the seventeenth century and ultimately succeeded in converting roughly 7 percent of the population to Catholicism. But the country, lacking the profitable commodities that drew European interest elsewhere, escaped colonization during the early years of Western expansion into Asia. Only a new set of political, geostrategic, and economic calculations drove France in the second half of the nineteenth century to claim the territories it dubbed Indochina. Emperor Napoléon III hoped that colonies in Asia would bathe his regime in imperial glory. Moreover, French leaders wished to keep pace with Great Britain, which had already established control of India, Burma, and Malaya and seemed poised for further growth.

Above all, though, French imperialism sprang from material motives. As the Industrial Revolution transformed the French economy, political and business elites looked abroad for raw materials and consumer markets necessary to keep French factories humming. By colonizing Indochina, they hoped not only to profit from the area but also to open a southern gateway to the even vaster resources and markets of China. All of these motives were suffused with the same conviction that had colored European forays into Asia, Africa, and the Western Hemisphere for centuries. As they tightened their grip, French colonizers declared that they were serving the Indochinese peoples by bringing material advancement and moral uplift—by performing, in short, a "civilizing mission."

France opened its bid to control Vietnam in 1858 and four years later scored its first major success. With no hope of resisting European military technology, the Vietnamese court in Hue ceded Saigon and three surrounding provinces to French rule. The colonizers soon gained control over the rest of southern Vietnam and in 1867 established the colony of Cochin China, which would become the most profitable part of Indochina. In the 1880s, the French forced the emperor to yield the rest of Vietnam and established the protectorates of Tonkin in the north and Annam along the central coast. Nominally, the emperor remained in charge in these areas, but colonial authorities wielded

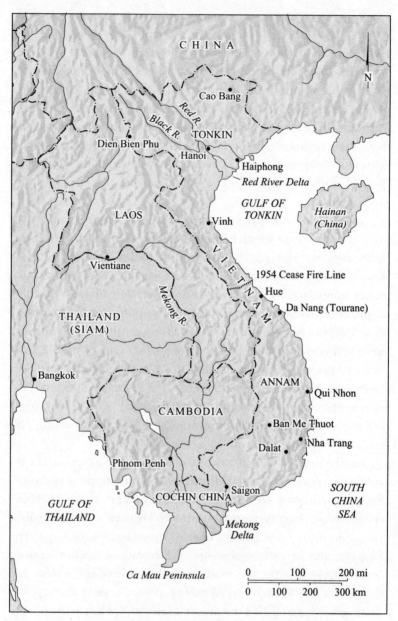

Map of Vietnam and surrounding territories in the era of French colonialism.

real power. The French government followed a similar approach to the west, establishing protectorates over Cambodia in 1863 and Laos in 1893.

Colonization profoundly altered life in Vietnam. A small number of Vietnamese benefited by serving the colonial authorities or by cashing in on the economic opportunities the French created. A new class of landlords, bankers, and merchants flourished, especially in the south, where the availability of land created a booming frontier economy for those with the resources to exploit it. As they amassed wealth, these privileged Vietnamese helped develop an opulent, Westernized lifestyle in the cities. They dressed in European clothes, drank wine, went bicycling, and sent their children to French schools.

For other Vietnamese, colonization brought hardship. To one small but influential group—the intellectuals, teachers, and imperial bureaucrats rooted in the old system of Confucian governance—the setback was more psychological than material. The subjugation of their nation by a vigorously confident, technologically advanced France caused Vietnamese elites to question the traditional political and philosophical underpinnings of their society. All that had once seemed sacred had been delegitimated, yielding what one Vietnamese author would later call a "national mood of pessimism."[2] Some of these elites, often benefiting from educational opportunities created by the French, began to consider ways of remaking Vietnamese society and overthrowing French control.

The peasantry, comprising more than 90 percent of the population, faced much more tangible problems. Colonial authorities frequently boasted of the roads, canals, bridges, and irrigation systems that they built in Indochina. But these developments served mainly to enrich French investors eager to transform Vietnam into an exporter of raw materials for the global market. The old system of subsistence farming, though hardly egalitarian, had

The wealth and splendor of central Saigon, depicted in this 1925 photograph, was a world apart from living conditions endured by many Vietnamese. (Postcard Collection, Vietnam Archive, Texas Tech University, VAPC0354)

provided most peasants with a secure existence by assuring access to small plots of lands. The new system imposed by France prized efficiency and profitability—objectives that could best be achieved by concentrating land in the hands of a small number of technologically advanced producers. French laws helped attain this goal by enabling wealthy entrepreneurs to claim land long cultivated by Vietnamese peasants and to purchase newly opened areas. New taxes imposed by colonial authorities, along with the establishment of French-controlled monopolies on salt, alcohol, and opium, also hurt small farmers. Unable to earn sufficient cash, many went into debt and ultimately were forced to sell their plots to wealthy speculators or planters.

Vietnam became one of the world's top exporters of rice, but this accomplishment came at a heavy cost. A majority of peasants became tenant farmers, sharecroppers, or agricultural wage laborers—workers, in other words, who farmed parcels owned by rich landowners. The disparity between the wealthy few and the impoverished multitude grew ever larger as a vicious cycle of indebtedness, desperation, and dependency took hold, often exacerbated by rampant corruption among the moneylenders and bureaucrats who milked the system for personal advantage. By the early twentieth century, less than 5 percent of the population of Cochin China, where the economic transformation was most extreme, owned more than half of the arable land.[3] Sketchy evidence suggests that per capita food consumption declined as production for the global market increased. "We had always had enough to eat, but then we got poorer every day," one peasant from central Vietnam remembered of French colonial rule.[4]

A few peasants managed to find jobs in the tiny new industrial sector set up by the French, but conditions there were no better. As miners, stevedores, factory hands, or rubber workers, Vietnamese faced long hours, miserable pay, and brutal discipline. So horrendous were conditions on Cochin Chinese rubber plantations that managers had to recruit workers in Tonkin and Annam, where potential laborers were less likely to know about the cruelty, disease, and malnourishment that awaited them. More than one in four rubber workers died on the harshest plantations. Runaways faced execution by torture, hanging, or stabbing. Life as a rubber worker was, according to a rough translation of the Vietnamese lament, "hell on earth."[5]

THE RISE OF VIETNAMESE NATIONALISM

If colonialism brought humiliation and deprivation, it also sowed the seeds of decolonization by giving rise to the vigorous nationalist movement that would shape Vietnamese politics in the twentieth century. The movement did not arise in a sudden, unified, or vigorous way. On the contrary, it showed little promise at first. The French military suppressed sporadic resistance, while anticolonial leaders lacked an agenda beyond restoration of the very social and political practices that the French conquest had discredited. By the turn of the century, little active opposition remained. Yet conditions were favorable for a powerful movement to take shape over time. The destruction of the old order left patriotic elites—self-conscious heirs to a tradition of struggle against foreign invaders—lacking a clear program and eager for new approaches to restore national independence and vigor. Meanwhile, the accumulation of grievances among ordinary Vietnamese meant that any appeal to establish a more just social order would likely resonate across the society as a whole. Over the decades leading up to 1945, this revolutionary potential slowly became reality.

The first crucial step came in the early twentieth century, when a new generation of nationalists began to look abroad for inspiration. The most influential was Phan Boi Chau, a scholar from central Vietnam who embraced Western rationalism and science as the keys to creating a robust, modern Vietnam. He questioned the old system of government based on loyalty to the monarch and imagined his homeland instead as a Western-style nation-state. In a stream of publications written from exile, Phan Boi Chau and his Modernization Society agitated tirelessly for the overthrow of French colonialism and the establishment of a constitutional monarchy or, as he came to prefer later in life, a republic. Another westward-looking nationalist, Phan Chu Trinh, considered such ideas impractical because, he believed, the Vietnamese were not yet ready to govern themselves. He contended that their best hope lay in demanding that France live up to its supposedly benevolent intentions by preparing Vietnam for independence over the long term.

Phan Boi Chau and Phan Chu Trinh had some success in rallying compatriots to support these new visions. During the First World War, a group of Saigon intellectuals inspired by Phan Chu Trinh's relatively moderate agenda launched the first openly nationalist organization in French-controlled Vietnam, the Constitutionalist Party, which demanded that colonial authorities grant greater economic and political opportunities for the indigenous population. A few years later, another group of elites dedicated to Phan Boi Chau's more radical ideas formed the clandestine Nationalist Party (Viet Nam Quoc Dan Dang), which advocated violent revolution against the French. But profound shortcomings ultimately prevented either group from seriously challenging French domination. For one thing, the two groups failed to overcome their differences and form a unified movement. Still more debilitating, they failed to extend their appeal beyond the narrow urban middle classes from which they sprang. Lacking sensitivity to rural conditions, these organizations did little to harness simmering peasant discontent. The narrowness of their social base also made it easy for the French police to monitor and suppress their activities.

These problems would be overcome only with the rise of yet another strand of nationalism—the one led by the most influential Vietnamese leader of all, the gaunt, ascetic firebrand best known as Ho Chi Minh. Over the course of his long career as nationalist agitator and then national leader, Ho showed a remarkable ideological flexibility and tactical genius that enabled him to succeed where earlier nationalists had failed. He celebrated Vietnam's history of resistance to foreigners even as he embraced foreign ideas and assistance. He created a sternly disciplined movement able to withstand French repression and crush his rivals even as he exuded personal warmth that inspired supporters to call him "Uncle Ho." Most important, he appealed to educated nationalists and urban radicals even as he mobilized the peasantry.

Born in a central Vietnamese village in 1890, Ho, then known as Nguyen Tat Thanh, imbibed fierce nationalism from his father, a mandarin who had resigned from the Confucian bureaucracy to protest the French takeover. Ho's boyhood home reverberated with patriotism and a yearning for new ideas about how to attain independence. His solution—to forge bonds between elites and peasants opposed to colonial domination—started to become clear in 1908, when he took action for the first time against French authorities. Early that year, peasants in several provinces demonstrated against rising taxes and coercive labor policies. As unrest spread, Ho jumped into the fray, eager to interact with the peasants and to translate their demands for local officials. Colonial police cracked down on the protest and ordered Ho's school to dismiss the "tall dark student" who had taken part.[6] Ho briefly found work as a teacher, but in 1911, harassed by French authorities and determined to see the world, he signed on to the crew of a freighter bound for Europe.

Ho Chi Minh spent the next three decades outside his native country, studying foreign societies, agitating for Vietnamese independence, and developing the ideas he would ultimately take back to Vietnam. His early travels took him to the United States, where he worked briefly as a pastry chef in Boston and a domestic servant in New York. He then relocated to Britain, where he became involved in labor union activities and probably learned about Karl Marx for the first time. Only after moving to France near the end of the First World War, however, did Ho Chi Minh step fully into the role of expatriate spokesman for Vietnamese anticolonialism. His breakthrough came in 1919, when leaders of the victorious Western powers gathered outside Paris to craft a new international order. Under the name of Nguyen Ai Quoc (Nguyen the Patriot), Ho Chi Minh led a group of Vietnamese exiles who petitioned the great powers to honor the principle of self-determination that U.S. President Woodrow Wilson had repeatedly avowed during the war. The relatively modest demands called not for immediate independence but for reforms including recognition of equal rights for Vietnamese and French people living in Vietnam and the inclusion of Vietnamese representatives in the French parliament.

The assembled presidents and prime ministers ignored the appeal, just as they ignored similar demands from groups representing other colonized peoples. Despite their florid liberal rhetoric, the great powers showed no interest in disbanding colonial empires. The whole episode catapulted Ho Chi Minh to the forefront of the Vietnamese nationalist movement but left him badly disappointed. For a brief moment, the Allied victory had seemed to herald a new era of democratization and self-determination around the globe. By 1920, this promise had come to nothing. The setback had a profound effect on Ho Chi Minh. Initially inspired by the liberal West, he now lamented its hypocrisy. Increasingly he looked for an alternative set of ideas to guide the fight against colonialism.

He found it in Leninism. Ho Chi Minh's leftward drift became clear in 1919, when he joined the French socialist party. He quickly grew discouraged by the party's lack of interest in colonial problems, however, and gravitated toward the more radical program of V. I. Lenin, mastermind of the Bolshevik Revolution that had established communist rule in Russia in 1917. Lenin wrote at great length about colonialism and even laid out a strategy for abolishing it. Like Marx, Lenin argued that full-fledged communist revolution could occur only in the most highly industrialized nations. Yet Lenin nonetheless saw anticolonial movements as crucial allies in the struggle to overthrow global capitalism and theorized that they could carry out revolutions of a particular kind. In peasant societies, Lenin called for the establishment of communist parties led by tiny groups of industrial workers and radical intellectuals. The parties would then carry out revolutions in two stages. First they would form alliances with disgruntled peasants and patriotic elites to overthrow colonial rule. Later they would break with their noncommunist allies and seize power in the name of international communism.

This was a revolutionary roadmap of the sort that Ho Chi Minh had been seeking. Lenin's vision not only endowed anticolonialism with transcendent historical importance but also meshed neatly with Ho's belief in the revolutionary potential of peasants. Captivated by Lenin's ideas, Ho helped found the French Communist Party in 1920 and over the next three years became its leading voice on colonial matters. He established an organization to promote cooperation among nationalists from different parts of the world and, having given up all hope of achieving progress through reformed colonial rule, for the first time published biting attacks on the French. All this work inevitably caught the attention of Soviet officials, who invited Ho to relocate to Moscow. He arrived in the capital of world communism in 1923.

Ho Chi Minh had a mixed experience in the Soviet Union—the start of an ambivalent relationship with communist powers that would continue over the rest of his life. On the one hand, Ho found golden opportunities to advance his study of Marxism-Leninism and to work for the Comintern, the bureaucracy established in 1919 to promote communist revolution globally. On the other, he encountered pervasive scorn among Soviet leaders for agricultural societies such as Vietnam. Marx's well-known dismissal of peasants as hopeless reactionaries, rather than Lenin's more optimistic view, prevailed among the communist functionaries with whom Ho interacted. At one Comintern meeting, Ho pledged to take "every opportunity" to remind his colleagues of colonial concerns. He confided to a friend, however, that he was just a "voice crying in the wilderness."[7]

Ho Chi Minh at a meeting of the French socialist party in 1920. (Library of Congress, LC-USZ62-62808)

Disappointed by attitudes in Moscow and aware of growing nationalist agitation in Indochina, Ho Chi Minh asked permission to return to Asia. The Comintern approved his request in mid-1924, dispatching him to the city of Guangzhou (Canton) in southeastern China. He wrote articles for a Soviet news agency and served as an interpreter for local Comintern representatives. But his primary mission was to establish a revolutionary organization among expatriate Vietnamese nationalists who had fled colonial repression in their home country. From these efforts arose Vietnam's first communist-oriented body, the Revolutionary Youth League. Although he took care to set up a small subgroup that might eventually form the kernel of a communist party, Ho Chi Minh saw no hope of inculcating the league's unsophisticated membership with full-fledged communist doctrine. Rather, as so often over the course of his life, he seamlessly blended communist

notions of social revolution with nationalist themes likely to resonate with a broad range of Vietnamese motivated mainly by anti-
French anger. Under Ho's charismatic leadership, the organization, founded in 1925, flourished and quickly extended its reach
into Vietnam itself. More than any other anticolonial group, its
appeal cut across socioeconomic and regional divides.

Within a few years, however, the organization fell into disar-
ray. The trouble began in 1927, when the Comintern made an
abrupt ideological shift, abandoning its support for broad co-
alitions of the type Ho Chi Minh preferred. Moscow ordered
communist movements to pursue more doctrinaire agendas
rooted narrowly in the interests of industrial workers and the
poorest peasants. The move fractured the Revolutionary Youth
League and marginalized Ho, who fell into deep disgrace in
Moscow. In 1930, new Vietnamese leaders freshly trained in the
Soviet Union established a new body, the Indochinese Communist Party (ICP), dedicated to the Comintern's policy.

An even bigger challenge for the communist movement
quickly ensued. Peasants throughout central Vietnam began
rioting against increasingly bleak economic conditions caused by
the Great Depression. For a moment, this seemed a promising
development for Vietnamese revolutionaries. In one province,
Nghe Tinh, radical peasants overthrew the local administration in
1930 and established governing committees they called "soviets"
in imitation of the workers' committees formed during the Bolshevik Revolution. But the episode quickly turned to disaster for
the revolutionaries. With fierce efficiency, French authorities put
down the rebellion and rounded up communists who had abetted
it. Ultimately the French executed or imprisoned 90 percent of
party leaders. The communist apparatus that had been pains-
takingly assembled over half a decade lay in ruins. Even Ho Chi
Minh, then living in the relative safety of British-controlled Hong
Kong, fell victim to European repression in 1931. Arrested during

a crackdown on political agitators, Ho spent several months in prison before being released and returning to Moscow.

WAR AND REVOLUTION

Communist fortunes in Vietnam improved only with the approach of the Second World War. The first step came in 1935 with a new shift by the Comintern. Alarmed by the rise of fascism in Germany and Japan, the Soviet government reverted to its policy of promoting alliances between communists and noncommunists around the world. The move not only relegitimated Ho Chi Minh, who had clung to his vision of a broad revolutionary alliance of communists and nationalists, but also generated unprecedented opportunities for communists to expand their influence in Vietnam. Under instructions from a leftist coalition that had come to power in France, the colonial government permitted the ICP to take part openly in Vietnamese political life. The party took full advantage, running candidates for local offices, forming self-help societies among industrial workers, and organizing intensively among the peasantry.

The outbreak of global war created still greater opportunities for Ho Chi Minh and his allies. Germany's crushing invasion of France in May 1940 badly weakened French power and prestige globally. In Indochina, this feebleness enabled Germany's ally, Japan, to extract humiliating military and economic concessions from the French colonial government. Although Tokyo permitted French authorities to maintain day-to-day administration, Japanese troops occupied all of Indochina by the end of 1941, making it part of the expanding Japanese empire in Southeast Asia. Many Vietnamese worried that they had merely exchanged one colonial master for another, but some saw a silver lining: the era of unchallenged European supremacy appeared to be at an end. Nationalist prospects brightened further in December 1941, when the attack on Pearl Harbor brought the United States into the war against Japan. The addition of vast American resources to the Allied side improved the odds that Japan would one day be defeated. Bold American declarations of self-determination and anticolonialism as key war aims also raised hopes among Vietnamese nationalists, many of whom continued to sympathize strongly with Western liberalism, that a U.S. victory would bring independence for Vietnam and other colonial territories.

It was clear, however, that none of this would come easy. In November 1941, French authorities demonstrated that they still had considerable fight left in them, decimating a communist-led rebellion in Cochin China. Communists fared little better in fighting the Japanese occupation. In Tonkin, Vietnamese guerrillas resisted briefly before fleeing into the mountains. Facing two powerful enemies, the ICP decided against direct confrontation, choosing instead to focus on political organizing while waiting for a propitious moment to resume military action.

Key strategic decisions came in May 1941 at an ICP Central Committee meeting in the secluded mountainside village of Pac Bo, near the Chinese border. Led by Ho Chi Minh, back in his homeland for the first time in three decades, the delegates submerged their party within a broad patriotic front called the League for the Independence of Vietnam (Viet Nam Doc Lap Dong Minh). The new organization, better known as the Viet Minh, was designed to garner support from a wide swath of the Vietnamese population by downplaying communist aims such as land redistribution and emphasizing instead patriotic themes that would appeal to radicals and moderates alike. This approach probably had another aim as well—to heighten the Viet Minh's appeal to the United States and other anticommunist powers that seemed likely to play a major role in determining who would govern postwar Vietnam. Still, the ICP sought to give the Viet

Minh some capacity to shape that outcome through its own action. Delegates embraced guerrilla warfare as the means by which the Vietnamese, when conditions allowed, would claim their independence.

The Viet Minh rapidly put this program into practice. Operating from its remote mountain headquarters in northern Vietnam, the new organization extended its influence southward from the Chinese border. True to the Pac Bo decisions, Viet Minh propaganda connected the forthcoming liberation struggle with the country's long patriotic traditions. "The sacred call of the fatherland is resounding in our ears, the ardent blood of our heroic predecessors is seething in our hearts," wrote Ho Chi Minh in one widely distributed declaration.[8] Ho also tended to the Viet Minh's diplomatic priorities. In 1943, he contacted U.S. intelligence operatives in southern China in hopes of forming an anti-Japanese partnership. Meanwhile, Vo Nguyen Giap, a history teacher turned military strategist, supervised the creation of guerrilla units, the nucleus of what Viet Minh leaders hoped would one day become a Vietnamese army.

All this preparation paid off in 1945, when rapid shifts in the global military balance created precisely the sort of opportunity that the Viet Minh had been seeking. In March, the Japanese government, alarmed by Allied advances in the Pacific, overthrew the French administration in Indochina. Japan established a nominally independent regime in Vietnam under the reigning emperor, Bao Dai. These events worked strongly in favor of the Viet Minh, however, because the disappearance of the French apparatus in the countryside enabled it to expand its influence as never before. The Japanese, facing imminent defeat, showed little interest in interfering. Greatly emboldened, revolutionary leaders decided that the moment had come to begin planning a popular uprising to coincide with Japan's final collapse. In its bid to win over the population, the Viet Minh benefited tremendously from its efforts to relieve a famine that killed more than one million Vietnamese in 1944 and 1945. Alone among the claimants to power, the Viet Minh sprang into action to make food available to starving peasants.

When Japan surrendered in early August, Vietnamese across the country rallied behind calls for insurrection and the establishment of an independent republic. "The decisive hour has struck for the destiny of our people," proclaimed Ho Chi Minh.[9] Although the Viet Minh enjoyed more support in northern and central Vietnam than in the south, it encountered little resistance as its influence spread village by village—the outpouring of nationalist fervor later dubbed the "August Revolution." Communist officials directed the proceedings in some places, but in others, despite later claims by communist historians, they struggled to keep up with the burgeoning insurrection and confronted challenges from rival nationalist organizations. Amid massive flag-waving demonstrations, the Viet Minh took charge in Hanoi on August 19, in Hué on August 23, and in Saigon on August 25. Five days later, Bao Dai reluctantly abdicated to the Viet Minh, thus conferring the "mandate of heaven"—the traditional notion of political legitimacy—onto Ho Chi Minh's movement. On September 2, 1945, Ho, the new president of the Vietnamese provisional government, climbed a hastily constructed platform in Hanoi's Ba Dinh Square to declare his nation's independence.

COLONIALISM
AND COLD WAR

HO CHI MINH'S DECLARATION OF VIETNAMESE independence was a peculiar piece of oratory. Ho began not by proclaiming the establishment of his new government. That came only in the closing sentences. Rather, he started by quoting the American Declaration of Independence. "All men are created equal," Ho Chi Minh stated. "They are endowed by their Creator with certain unalienable Rights; among these are Life, Liberty, and the pursuit of Happiness."[1] Ho's choice of words reflected his calculation that the fate of his new nation, the Democratic Republic of Vietnam (DRV), depended crucially on the United States, which had almost single-handedly defeated Japan and seemed in 1945 to control the destiny of Asia. By invoking the principles that Americans ostensibly held dear, he hoped to persuade U.S. leaders to embrace the newly proclaimed Vietnamese state.

The gambit failed miserably. Washington ignored the appeal and then stood aside as France launched efforts to resubjugate Indochina. But Ho Chi Minh was correct in his larger judgment:

foreign nations would play decisive roles in determining what became of the DRV. Between 1945 and 1954, the mightiest countries in the world, spurred by the intensification of the Cold War,
intervened powerfully in Vietnam to destroy—or sustain—Ho Chi
Minh's government. The United States, the Soviet Union, and
communist China came to see fighting between France and the
Viet Minh, at root a renewed struggle over colonialism, as a vital
front in the global confrontation between democratic capitalism
and international communism. For their part, meanwhile, DRV
leaders, no mere bystanders as their nation's fate was determined
by others, learned to exploit international tensions to advance
their cause.

THE PATH TO WAR

As it attempted to consolidate its authority in the fall of 1945, the
Vietnamese government confronted serious challenges. Its control was shaky in the south, where much of the population opposed the DRV and the communist movement had yet to recover
from French repression during the Second World War. The
government also faced a severe economic crisis. But the biggest
threat came from abroad. In the near term, two new occupiers,
Britain and China, seemed to pose the most serious dangers. By
agreement among the Allied powers, British forces entered
southern Vietnam at the end of World War II to disarm Japanese
soldiers, while Chinese forces performed the same function in
the north. The occupiers were not supposed to interfere in local
politics, but both Britain and China—the latter controlled by the
vigorously anticommunist Nationalist government led by Chiang
Kai-shek—seemed certain to create problems for the DRV.

In the longer term, the main danger came from France. Despite
debilitating weaknesses caused by four years of war and occupa-

tion by Germany, the French government was determined to restore colonial rule over Indochina. Across the political spectrum, French leaders believed that their country could recover its power and prestige only by reclaiming its empire. Indochina held particular importance because of its economic value and its great distance from Europe. Together with possessions in Africa and the Middle East, it enabled France to claim the status of a truly global power.

Leaders of the DRV believed that their best hope of fending off these threats lay in finding foreigners to side with them. The pickings, however, were slim. The Soviet government, consumed with European priorities and suspicious of Ho Chi Minh's independent streak, had little interest in the new Vietnamese state. The Chinese communists were preoccupied by their own struggle for power within China. India and other decolonizing Asian nations were too weak to provide anything more than moral support. Only the United States seemed a promising ally. When he appealed to Americans in his independence address, Ho Chi Minh had reason to believe that Washington might respond sympathetically. Throughout the Second World War, the U.S. government had frequently declared that it was fighting for the principle of national self-determination. Then, in the final weeks of the war, agents of the U.S. Office of Strategic Services, the forerunner to the Central Intelligence Agency, had cooperated with Viet Minh forces conducting anti-Japanese operations in the Tonkinese mountains. The agents provided weapons and encouraged Ho Chi Minh's belief that Washington would view his movement favorably.

Viet Minh leaders had no way of knowing the full extent of American misgivings about French rule in Indochina. During the war, U.S. president Franklin D. Roosevelt had repeatedly, albeit always secretly, heaped scorn on France and demanded that Vietnam be set on the road to independence once the fighting ended. "After 100 years of French rule in Indochina, the inhabitants are worse off than they had been before," Roosevelt exclaimed to Soviet leader Josef Stalin in 1943.[2] Roosevelt's solution was not immediate independence. Like most Americans of his generation, he believed that the Vietnamese and other nonwhite peoples around the world lacked the ability to govern themselves. Rather, he proposed that the great powers establish a trusteeship—temporary control by benevolent foreign powers—to prepare Vietnam for eventual independence.

The United States failed, however, to follow through on Roosevelt's anticolonial impulses. That failure fit with a long pattern of American behavior. Despite its rhetoric, the United States had seldom supported revolutionary movements in the colonial world and in the 1890s had even acquired colonies of its own. But the collapse of Roosevelt's trusteeship scheme also resulted from specific developments in the final months of the Second World War. Roosevelt's death in April 1945 silenced the most powerful voice in favor of the plan and cleared the way for a new president, Harry S Truman, who had little interest in colonial controversies. Meanwhile, major shifts in the international climate pushed American policymakers to take a more favorable view of French claims to Indochina. The intensification of bitter civil war in China made U.S. leaders anxious to shore up reliable sources of authority elsewhere in Asia. More important, rising tensions with the Soviet Union over the postwar settlement in Europe left Washington wary of doing anything that might alienate France, which Washington increasingly viewed as a valuable partner in opposing Soviet expansionism. In particular, U.S. officials worried that any move to end French rule in Southeast Asia would unsettle French politics and thereby strengthen the French Communist Party.

Eager to cement good relations with Paris, Truman made clear to French leaders in May 1945 that Washington had no intention of opposing the restoration of colonialism in Indochina. To be sure, the U.S. administration stopped short of declaring outright support for the reimposition of French rule. American policymakers were too worried about alienating Asian nationalists to go that far. But U.S. neutrality greatly benefited France by removing the biggest potential impediment to the recovery of colonialism in Indochina.

Once the Second World War ended, the French government seized that opportunity. The task of reimposing French authority was relatively simple in the south, where British occupation forces, eager to support fellow European colonialists, provided crucial assistance. British troops facilitated a French coup against the Viet Minh administration in Saigon in September 1945 and then helped French troops, many of them hastily shipped from Europe, extend their control throughout Cochin China. In the north, Chinese occupation troops were far less friendly to French aims and barred colonial authorities from entering the area for several months, giving DRV leaders invaluable breathing space to expand and consolidate their control. French troops returned only after France signed an agreement in February 1946 making sweeping concessions to China.

In addition to granting China economic privileges in Vietnam, French negotiators bent to Chinese insistence that they reach a compromise settlement with the Viet Minh. Many French officials wanted to crush the DRV militarily. But when the Chinese government, wary of becoming embroiled in Franco–Viet Minh fighting, insisted on a more peaceful course, French leaders accepted negotiations with Ho Chi Minh as the price of getting Chinese troops out of the country as quickly as possible.[3] In Hanoi, meanwhile, DRV leaders preferred talks as the best way to head off a war they doubted they could win. Their willingness to hold talks was, in fact, just one of several steps designed to placate the DRV's many adversaries by displaying moderation. The DRV government called for free elections and in November 1945 disbanded the communist party to allay fears of communism inside and outside the country, although the party continued to operate secretly.

Ho Chi Minh and French representative Jean Sainteny struck a deal on March 6, 1946. France promised to recognize Vietnam as a self-administering "free state" within a reconfigured imperial framework to be known as the French Union. In return, the DRV permitted France to station fifteen thousand troops in northern Vietnam and to maintain its economic and cultural interests in the country. The thorniest problem turned out to be the status of Vietnam's southernmost region, Cochin China, which the DRV regarded as an integral part of Vietnam but Paris considered a separate colony legally bound to France. The two sides agreed to settle the matter later through a plebiscite.

The Ho-Sainteny agreement, intended as a mere starting point for further negotiations, turned out to be the high point of Franco-Vietnamese amity. In both countries, the deal came under sharp attack from extremists who opposed compromise. By the time follow-up talks convened in France in the summer of 1946, the mood among the negotiators had soured considerably. The main bone of contention remained Cochin China. Conservative French leaders in Paris and Saigon, shocked by the prospect of losing direct control over the colony, torpedoed the plebiscite plan. Disgusted, the Vietnamese delegation went home. Only Ho Chi Minh stayed in Paris in hopes of avoiding war. In September, he signed a "modus vivendi" that merely committed both sides to keep talking.

That agreement accomplished nothing. While Vietnamese militants criticized Ho Chi Minh for selling out to the French, Viet Minh commander Vo Nguyen Giap prepared the ragtag Vietnamese army for action. French forces in Indochina also braced for the military showdown that many French officials had long wanted. Indeed, the French high commissioner for Indochina, Admiral Thierry d'Argenlieu, did much to provoke a war by attempting to roll back DRV sovereignty whenever possible. Sporadic skirmishing gave way to a major clash on November 20, 1946, when a dispute over collection of customs duties at Haiphong escalated into urban combat that cost thousands of lives. A month later, Hanoi exploded into violence when Viet Minh troops attacked French soldiers who were spoiling for a fight. After intense combat, the French army forced the DRV government to flee its capital city. But Vietnamese leaders pledged to carry on. "Those who have rifles will use their rifles; those who have swords will use their swords," declared Ho Chi Minh. "Those who have no swords will use spades, hoes or sticks."[4]

INTERNATIONALIZATION

Vastly superior in arms and mobility, French forces scored quick successes. Colonial troops—an assortment of army regulars, Foreign Legionnaires, and Vietnamese conscripts—captured most key cities of northern and central Vietnam in the first weeks of fighting. In fall 1947, a major offensive inflicted heavy Vietnamese casualties and nearly captured DRV leaders headquartered in the Tonkinese mountains.

These achievements did not, however, add up to victory. On the contrary, DRV forces withstood the initial onslaught and developed considerable strengths of their own. Most crucially, they garnered broad support in the countryside, where the brutality of French military operations deepened old anticolonial anger. Viet Minh forces found a steady stream of recruits and maximized their limited firepower through skillful guerrilla operations. Meanwhile, DRV leaders settled on a military strategy that rationalized their early setbacks and provided a blueprint for future success. Drawing inspiration from writings by the Chinese revolutionary Mao Zedong, Vietnamese strategists outlined a three-stage approach. First, Viet Minh forces would make a tactical retreat to the northern mountains; second, they would undertake limited attacks designed to exploit their advantages; third, after building up their strength, they would initiate a "general offensive" to retake the cities.

By 1948 the war had settled into a stalemate characterized by a pattern that would prevail for years to come. The French army controlled the cities and numerous fortified posts, while the Viet Minh dominated the rural areas in between. French troops had little difficulty extending their control into the countryside when they wished. As soon as they withdrew to their bases, however, the Viet Minh quickly reasserted its authority. In countless villages, Viet Minh influence deepened as activists spread their ideas, harassed their enemies, and established governing bodies that redistributed land, collected taxes, and gathered supplies to sustain guerrilla operations against the French. And yet the revolutionaries, armed with a hodgepodge of crude and outdated weapons, stood little chance of converting their achievements into overall victory.

The problem for both French and DRV leaders lay in finding a way to break out of this deadlock. The French strategy, developed as the war ground on between 1947 and 1949, had two prongs. First, officials in Paris sought to draw popular support away from the DRV. The French government declared that it would no longer talk to Ho Chi Minh, whom it dismissed as an unredeemable communist. It then installed Bao Dai, the former emperor, as titular head of an alternative Vietnamese government to which France gradually ceded a degree of independence. Although French officials knew Bao Dai's reputation as an unprincipled dilettante, they hoped he could build on his following among conservative nationalists, Catholics, and other groups to challenge Ho Chi Minh for leadership of Vietnamese national-ism. On March 8, 1949, Bao Dai and French president Vincent Auriol signed agreements establishing the "Associated State of Vietnam." France followed the same approach in Cambodia and Laos, establishing "Associated States" under local monarchs later in 1949.

The second dimension of the French strategy was to attract international support for the new Vietnamese state and, by ex-tension, the French war effort. Although Britain remained a strong ally, most of the world chastised France for going to war in Vietnam—a manifestation, the critics complained, of an outdated colonial mentality. Defiant French leaders initially hoped they could ignore foreign condemnation. As the fighting continued, however, they confronted a major problem: France was running out of the financial and military resources necessary to wage a major war while living up to other commitments around the world. France could keep fighting, the government concluded, only if it obtained help from abroad. Above all, it wanted aid from the United States, by far the world's most powerful nation. To persuade U.S. officials, French diplomats stressed a theme they believed would resonate in Washington. France, they declared, was waging not a colonial war but a war against communism.

Leaders of the DRV followed a parallel diplomatic approach as they struggled to break the stalemate in their favor. Ho Chi Minh's strenuous efforts in 1945 and 1946 to cultivate sympathy abroad had come to nothing, leaving the DRV without any allies when war broke out. The revolutionaries lacked not only inter-national legitimacy but also sources of advanced military equip-ment. Feeling dangerously isolated, Viet Minh leaders appealed anew for foreign assistance. Ho left the door ajar for cooperation with the United States. Increasingly, though, DRV leaders looked to the Soviet Union as the most likely source of help. Eager to win Soviet favor, they placed new emphasis on their dedication to international communism—a trend that culminated in 1951 with the reestablishment of a full-fledged communist party, now called the Vietnam Workers' Party.

Both France and the DRV achieved spectacular success in their efforts to obtain foreign backing. Between 1947 and 1950, first the United States and then the Soviet Union and communist China concluded that they must intervene with political, economic, and military assistance in order to serve their most urgent geostrategic priorities. At this crucial turning point, the war in Vietnam assumed a dual character that would persist for years to come: it was simultaneously a colonial struggle and a Cold War confrontation.

In the United States, various considerations led the Truman administration to abandon the neutral position that it had adopted in 1945 toward French aims in Vietnam. For one thing, the solidification of Soviet rule in Eastern Europe, culminating in the communist takeover of Czechoslovakia in 1948, heightened American eagerness to bolster France. The logic became even more compelling in 1949, when France joined the United States and ten other nations in establishing the North Atlantic Treaty Organization. It was clear to U.S. officials that France could play its role as a bulwark within the alliance only if Washington helped ease the financial and military burdens that Paris bore in Vietnam.

Developments within Asia also led the Truman administration to shift course. In 1948, communist insurrections broke out in Burma and Malaya. Suddenly the DRV war effort appeared to be part of a general communist offensive in Southeast Asia. Some U.S. officials insisted that Vietnamese revolutionaries were driven more by nationalist than communist goals. For most policymakers, however, subtle distinctions between nationalism and communism faded from view as the dangers of Soviet expansion came into focus. Washington believed that communist control over Southeast Asia's abundant natural resources would greatly enhance

Soviet power worldwide. Conversely, it feared that a communist takeover would cripple Britain and Japan, nations that relied heavily on those same resources to rebuild their war-devastated economies.

Rising anxiety about Southeast Asia exploded into an all-consuming sense of crisis in the summer of 1949, when Mao Zedong's communist forces triumphed in the Chinese civil war and took power in Beijing. From that moment, U.S. officials believed, it was only a matter of time before the new People's Republic of China, weak from internal conflict but bristling with revolutionary ardor, began sending aid across its southern borders to the DRV and other communist movements. If Southeast Asia was to be saved, it seemed, the United States had to act quickly. Officials had little difficulty agreeing on a basic plan. Over the previous few years, Washington had settled on a general approach for resisting communism in Europe. Under the containment policy embraced in 1946, the Truman administration had decided not to challenge communism where it already had taken hold but to block its further expansion. Under the 1947 Truman Doctrine, the administration had pledged to aid foreigners actively fighting communist encroachment. With communism threatening to spill beyond Chinese borders, the moment seemed to have arrived to extend these solutions to Asia.

The Soviet Union and China took longer to line up behind the DRV, but the result was no less of an internationalization of the war on the communist side. Stalin's attitude toward colonial areas started to shift in 1947, when he abandoned hope of achieving his objectives in Europe through cooperation with France and other colonial powers. In a landmark speech that paralleled the Truman Doctrine, Stalin's second in command, Andrei Zhdanov, declared that the world had split into two camps and that the communists would support "patriotic elements" fighting colonialism.[5] At the same time, communist leaders around the world established a new bureaucracy, the Communist Information Bureau, aimed at spreading revolution. Still, Southeast Asia ranked low on Stalin's list of priorities and lay too far away for Moscow to achieve much in practice.

The communist victory in China brought tremendous new opportunities. In Moscow, Stalin became suddenly enthusiastic about communist expansion throughout Asia. He told visiting Chinese officials that the focus of world revolution had shifted to the East, and he proposed a division of labor with Beijing: China would take the lead in promoting revolution in Asia while the Soviet Union focused on Europe. That scheme fit well with Mao's budding determination to help communists in neighboring areas. For various reasons, Mao was particularly interested in the DRV. He wanted Vietnamese assistance in consolidating control in the part of China nearest Vietnam. He also probably felt personal affinity for Ho Chi Minh, a fellow Asian communist who had endured similar hardships over a lifetime of revolutionary activism. Mao may even have relished the prospect of restoring China's traditional role as protector of Vietnam. Most of all, though, Mao wished to help the DRV for the same reason he wanted to help communists in other Asian territories: spreading revolution abroad promised to help consolidate communist rule within China by validating his government's claims to represent a new brand of revolutionary dynamism that could inspire other parts of the world.[6]

The DRV's leaders warmly welcomed the Chinese communist victory, which seemed likely to help them, at long last, overcome their isolation from the communist bloc and obtain material help from abroad. They were not disappointed. When Ho Chi Minh requested assistance, Mao readily agreed, and on January 18, 1950, China became the first nation to grant diplomatic recognition to the DRV government. The Soviet Union and its communist satellites followed suit a few days later. "It is the duty of those countries

French Foreign Legion soldiers capture a Viet Minh fighter, along with a flag bearing the communist hammer and sickle, near Saigon in November 1950. (AP Images)

that have achieved the victory of their own revolution to support peoples who are still conducting the just struggle for liberation," one senior Chinese leader, Liu Shaoqi, told a DRV delegation visiting Beijing. The Chinese government quickly promised to send unlimited assistance.[7]

Communist recognition of the DRV provided the final push that drove many Western nations to swallow their doubts about Bao Dai's rickety regime and back France. On February 7, the Truman administration formally opened relations with the Associated State of Vietnam, and several U.S. allies took the same step in the following days. Washington soon promised to send military and economic aid to help France carry on the war. By early spring, the bipolar global order had been fully superimposed onto the conflict in Vietnam, with Ho Chi Minh and Bao Dai embodying sharply different visions of Vietnam's postcolonial future. The struggle over those visions would divide the Vietnamese and the international community for a quarter century to come.

THE END OF THE FRENCH ERA

The outbreak of the Korean War at the end of June 1950 strengthened American determination to back the French. Suddenly, with the communist invasion of South Korea, Vietnam seemed more imperiled than ever. The Truman administration readily concluded that the United States, facing heavy military burdens in Europe and Korea, could not possibly send its own troops into Vietnam. But it opened the aid spigot ever more widely. Washington sent aircraft, tanks, artillery, naval vessels, small weapons, ammunition, communications gear, and other equipment. By the end of 1952, the United States bore more than one-third of the cost of the war. Meanwhile, Washington spent millions of dollars on economic and technical assistance aimed at strengthening the Bao Dai government and broadening its appeal among the Vietnamese population.

American aid enabled the French army to wage war in increasingly bloody and destructive ways but produced no breakthrough. In fact, the tide turned suddenly against France in the fall of 1950. Drawing on Chinese advice and supplies, the Viet Minh drove the French army from its fortifications along the Chinese frontier—a major blow that opened new avenues for Sino-Vietnamese cooperation. Beijing helped revamp the DRV economy and administrative apparatus while sending greater quantities of military aid that enabled Hanoi to transform its guerrilla force into a modern army capable of taking the battle to the French with unprecedented ferocity. In the political arena, meanwhile, Bao Dai gained a trickle of support but fell far short of rivaling Ho Chi Minh. "No one here respected Emperor Bao Dai," recalled one peasant from central Vietnam. "He was just a playboy and a puppet of the Westerners."[8]

To American policymakers, that sort of attitude was the nub of the problem in Vietnam. Washington reasoned that ordinary Vietnamese would abandon Ho Chi Minh only if they came to see Bao Dai as a genuine nationalist. Accordingly, the Truman administration applied strong pressure on the French government to cede greater independence and to follow through on pledges to permit the State of Vietnam to establish a robust army of its own. Such pressure yielded vague promises to enhance Vietnamese autonomy and modest steps to beef up Bao Dai's Vietnamese National Army. But none of this came close to satisfying U.S. demands. Simmering tension between ostensible allies exposed a fundamental contradiction in the Franco-American partnership. Whereas U.S. leaders viewed the war principally as a Cold War struggle against communism, their French counterparts saw it primarily as a campaign to preserve colonial prerogatives. To grant full independence to Vietnam would, for France, undercut the basic reason for fighting.

Washington saw no alternative but to tolerate recalcitrance on the colonial issue. Indeed, the French government held considerable leverage over Washington. As French leaders pointed out to their American counterparts, France could withdraw from Vietnam—and leave the whole mess in U.S. hands—if Washington pushed them too hard. Paris found additional advantage in U.S. eagerness to wage the Cold War assertively in Europe. The United States required French support to move ahead with one of its highest international priorities, the establishment of a multinational military force known as the European Defense Community. Many French leaders dragged their feet on establishing the force as a way to ensure that Washington kept sending aid to Indochina.

But French manipulation was hardly necessary to keep American assistance flowing. Sharply escalating East-West tensions during the Korean War left U.S. officials more determined than ever to fight communism globally, no matter what the cost. The Truman administration also felt strong pressure from its political opponents in the Republican Party. Spearheaded by Wisconsin Senator Joseph McCarthy, Republicans mercilessly attacked Democrats for "losing" China to communism in 1949. In the heyday of McCarthyism, administration officials had little doubt that a communist triumph in Vietnam would expose them to fierce new attacks.

American spirits improved sharply in December 1950, when Paris appointed the charismatic General Jean de Lattre de Tassigny as high commissioner and commander of French forces in Indochina. The highly decorated, battle-scarred soldier exuded confidence and energy as he toured Indochina, proclaiming, "We shall not yield another inch of territory!"[9] He also gratified Washington by pledging to "perfect" Vietnamese independence. Most important, he delivered on the battlefield, smashing a major Viet Minh offensive in the Red River Delta in early 1951. Yet not even de Lattre could achieve lasting results. When he tried to follow up his initial victory, French forces suffered a major defeat. As Franco-U.S. relations soured again, the general left Vietnam in late 1951. He died of cancer the following year.

French fortunes declined further in 1952 and 1953 despite continued military buildup. Forces under French command increased to more than five hundred thousand troops, and U.S. aid grew so prodigiously that it accounted for 80 percent of the cost of the war by early 1954. In most respects, though, the DRV held the upper hand. The Viet Minh kept pace with the increase in French forces, growing to almost three hundred thousand soldiers by the end of 1952 and offsetting U.S. aid with foreign help of its own. Chinese deliveries increased from about four hundred tons of equipment per month in the early phase of Sino-DRV cooperation to at least ten thousand tons a month by 1954.[10] Closely supervised by Chinese advisers, the Viet Minh developed an efficient force increasingly capable of directly challenging the French army. French control shrank to bands of territory surrounding the biggest cities. Beijing refused DRV requests for combat troops but nevertheless stationed more than two hundred fifty thousand troops near the Vietnamese border, a deployment intended to reassure the Viet Minh and stir worry in the West that the Vietnam conflict might escalate into a major international war.[11]

An even more serious threat to the French war effort emerged within France. As fighting dragged on, popular support dropped precipitously. The fighting constituted a debilitating drain on the sclerotic French economy, aggravating social tensions and undermining France's ability to pursue its priorities in Europe. The war also took a devastating human toll. By the end of 1952, more than fifty thousand soldiers from France and the French empire were dead, missing, or captured—seemingly senseless losses in a brutal conflict nicknamed "the dirty war" (*la sale guerre*). Pressure steadily mounted on the French government to negotiate an end to the fighting.

Viet Minh gains and French war weariness stoked deep anxiety in Washington, where a new president, Dwight D. Eisenhower, was no less determined than his predecessor to prevent a communist victory. Eisenhower had won the White House partly through promises to wage the Cold War more assertively. Accordingly, the administration applied strong pressure on France to reinvigorate the war in Vietnam with bolder political and military moves. The French had to prosecute the war "to the maximum extent of their capabilities," the U.S. Joint Chiefs of Staff insisted.[12] Anxious to act before public support collapsed within France, Paris responded with an ambitious program that included fuller independence for Bao Dai's State of Vietnam, further expansion of

French forces, and a more aggressive military strategy under a new commander, General Henri Navarre. The Eisenhower administration agreed to pay $385 million to implement the "Navarre Plan."

As in the past, Americans were disappointed. Navarre had to scuttle his offensive plans when his rival, General Vo Nguyen Giap, launched powerful attacks of his own. On the diplomatic front, meanwhile, developments were even more worrisome to Washington, which feared that military failures would lead France to sue for peace. That possibility grew much more likely when international negotiations put an end to the Korean War in July 1953. Encouraged by that example, Premier Joseph Laniel announced in October that he was open to similar talks to seek peace in Indochina. Momentum for talks increased further when the Soviet and Chinese governments declared their willingness to take part. Ho Chi Minh, eager to end a destructive war and probably confident of a favorable settlement, added his approval in November.

With negotiations increasingly probable, French and Viet Minh commanders sought to improve their governments' bargaining positions by landing decisive blows on the battlefield. They focused their attention above all on Dien Bien Phu, a remote valley in northwestern Vietnam near the Laotian border. Navarre set up a major fortified base there to block an anticipated Viet Minh invasion of Laos and to lure Giap into a major battle. Confident that it possessed overwhelming firepower, the French command conceded the mountains encircling Dien Bien Phu to the enemy and dug in for a fight on the valley floor.

The French got their wish—but not the result they expected. On March 13, 1954, Viet Minh leaders, eager for a big battle, launched a massive assault against the base and quickly overran outlying fortifications. Giap's success stemmed from a tremendous logistical achievement over the previous months. More than two

Ho Chi Minh (center) and other officials of the Democratic Republic of Vietnam plan the Dien Bien Phu campaign in early 1954. Military commander Vo Nguyen Giap stands at the far right, while Pham Van Dong, another key revolutionary leader, stands second from the left. (Douglas Pike Collection, Vietnam Archive, Texas Tech University, VAS000067)

hundred fifty thousand Viet Minh laborers, roughly half of them women known collectively as the "long-haired army," had lugged Soviet-made artillery and other equipment into the rugged mountains around Dien Bien Phu.[13] More than fifty thousand well-armed DRV troops surrounded the garrison below when the assault began. Within two weeks, they had destroyed the French airstrip, isolating the twelve-thousand-man garrison from reinforcement. The whole base lay in jeopardy.

The siege of Dien Bien Phu became a media sensation around the world. The fate of Indochina, and perhaps all of Southeast Asia, seemed to hang in the balance. In strictly military terms, the battle was not decisive, for it engaged only a small fraction of

French forces in Vietnam. But in a larger sense the grandiose claims about the battle's significance rang true. Defeat was certain to cement the French government's desire for peace and to strengthen the communist hand in negotiations set to open in May in Geneva, Switzerland.

Desperate to keep France fighting, the Eisenhower administration considered launching U.S. air strikes against Viet Minh positions. A few U.S. commanders even broached the use of nuclear weapons. For a mix of reasons, however, the administration rejected intervention of any kind. Washington officials continued to doubt French willingness to address basic political problems. They worried, too, that American intervention could not be kept limited. "Once the flag is committed," warned several members of Congress, "the use of land forces would surely follow."[14] Fresh off three grueling years of war in Korea, few Americans wanted to risk another major embroilment in Asia. American caution deepened when Britain, wary of igniting a major war in Southeast Asia, and other countries rebuffed Eisenhower's proposal for multinational military action in Vietnam. It was clear that if the United States intervened, it would do so alone. Unwilling to jump by itself into the unknown, Washington stood aside as the Viet Minh overran Dien Bien Phu on May 7, 1954.

An Anguished Peace

On May 7, 1954, French defenses crumbled at Dien Bien Phu. "C'est fini," sighed Major Jean Nicolas, commander of the last bunker to fall.[1] Unquestionably, the battle, a fifty-five-day siege waged in a soup of mud and blood, was over. So too, it seemed, was the war. The French premier appealed for a ceasefire on May 8, the same day that international talks on Indochina opened in Geneva.

No one could say what the negotiations might yield. The rout at Dien Bien Phu suggested that the Democratic Republic of Vietnam had won the war and deserved to rule a unified Vietnam. As in the period after the Second World War, however, Ho Chi Minh's regime had to reckon with numerous foreign powers eager to shape Indochina's destiny in pursuit of their own geopolitical agendas. Above all, the United States, having spent nearly $3 billion to defeat the DRV, made clear its hostility to communist ambitions in Vietnam.

In the end, the great powers reached a compromise at Geneva that suited their interests. The division of Vietnam into communist and noncommunist halves enabled Washington, Moscow, and Beijing to end a dangerous and draining conflict while ensuring that neither East nor West would wholly dominate Indochina. The problem was that the agreement, so sensible to diplomats concerned with the Cold War balance of power, did not produce a sustainable basis for peace in Vietnam. Rather, it yielded a few years of restive calm—a period of "anguished peace," as French General Paul Ely called it—during which old grievances and new hostilities boiled just beneath the surface.[2]

THE GENEVA SETTLEMENT

The outcome at Dien Bien Phu emboldened the DRV delegation to the Geneva talks to make an ambitious opening bid that revealed communist aims not just in Vietnam but also in Laos and Cambodia. Delegation leader Pham Van Dong demanded international recognition of the independence and unity of all three Indochinese states, withdrawal of foreign troops, and locally supervised elections for new governments. He also insisted that Laotian and Cambodian communists be seated as official participants in the Geneva meetings.

The Western powers had different ideas. The French government hoped to hold onto a significant degree of influence, at least in the south. But the fiercest opposition to the DRV's agenda came from the United States, where policymakers remained deeply wary of communist expansion in Asia. Indeed, during the Dien Bien Phu siege, Eisenhower had spoken more forcefully than any American leader ever had about the stakes in Indochina. "The possible consequences of the loss are just incalculable to the free world," stated the president, who warned of a "falling domino principle."[3] If the communists captured Indochina, he asserted, they would soon take Thailand, Malaya, and Indonesia and might even threaten Japan, the Philippines, and Australia.

Fearful that the battlefield situation would give the communists the upper hand at the conference table, the Eisenhower administration barely consented to take part in the talks at all. Secretary of State John Foster Dulles asserted that the United States would participate merely as an "interested nation," not as a "principal," and he refused to shake hands with the head of the Chinese delegation, Prime Minister Zhou Enlai.[4] Meanwhile, the administration revived the possibility of multinational intervention in Indochina to keep the war going. As negotiators met in Geneva, American and French commanders secretly drew up plans for U.S. air strikes.

Such scheming came to nothing, however, as American leaders once again confronted a disappointing reality: their Western allies were increasingly committed to the negotiations. The British government, nervous about its declining international status, embraced its role alongside the Soviet Union as co-chair of the Geneva meetings. For its part, the French government discarded any idea of renewed war after a leadership change in mid-June 1954. The new premier, Pierre Mendès-France, a longtime critic of the way the war had been fought, promised to reach a peace settlement by July 20 and vowed to resign if he was not successful.

Ironically, the good news for Washington came not from its allies but its adversaries. As the talks progressed, the communist powers made clear they were open to a compromise. China and the Soviet Union agreed to a French suggestion to divide Vietnam temporarily, with the DRV administering only the northern half of the country and Bao Dai's government administering the south. They also accepted noncommunist solutions for Laos and Cambodia. Several considerations drove Beijing and Moscow to accept these terms. Most important, both governments feared that a confrontational approach might push Washington to intervene directly in Indochina, igniting a new war with the potential to explode into a major conflagration. In this way, Dulles's combativeness resonated even after he had given up hope of military action. Beijing, worn out by the Korean War and eager to focus on domestic priorities, wanted no part of new fighting. By demonstrating moderation, moreover, Chinese leaders hoped to overcome their international isolation. In Moscow, meanwhile, new leaders who emerged after Stalin's death in 1953 wanted better relations with the West in order to concentrate on the Soviet Union's vast internal problems.

The challenge for Moscow and Beijing was to win DRV acceptance of the compromise. Many Viet Minh leaders were undoubtedly furious about the moderation of their patrons, but they grudgingly accepted Zhou Enlai's warnings that the United States might intervene directly if the talks collapsed. Under Chinese questioning, General Giap said that he might need three to five more years to defeat the French even if the United States did not enter the war. The best chance for communist control over all Vietnam, DRV leaders conceded, was to accept partition and to work for unification later, after the American danger had subsided. Having met personally with Zhou Enlai on these matters, Ho Chi Minh set about convincing skeptical compatriots to live with the emerging settlement.[5]

Early on the morning of July 21, the final deal was struck at Geneva—an agreement that neatly balanced the interests of the great powers but left Vietnam's future uncertain. The country would be divided at the seventeenth parallel, with French-led forces withdrawing to the south and Viet Minh units moving to the north. The accord called for reunification of the country through nationwide elections in 1956. It required little imagination, however, to foresee that those elections, which would necessitate the cooperation of bitter Vietnamese rivals, might not occur. Indeed, the Geneva agreement recognized that danger, specifying that the dividing line between the two "regroupment zones" must not be seen as a permanent "political or territorial boundary." The accord further prohibited either half of Vietnam from joining international alliances and barred outsiders from introducing military equipment or establishing bases.[6]

Right-wing critics in the United States, focusing on the "loss" of northern Vietnam, assailed the deal as a giveaway to the communists. Fearing political damage, the Eisenhower administration refused to sign the Geneva Accords, limiting itself to a frosty unilateral declaration that merely took note of the deal and pledged not to "disturb" it through force or the threat of force.[7] Behind the scenes, though, administration officials were not wholly disappointed with an outcome far better than the military situation had led them to expect. "Diplomacy," boasted the chief U.S.

Victorious Viet Minh soldiers parade through the streets of Hanoi on October 9, 1954, reclaiming the city according to the terms of the Geneva agreement signed earlier in the year. (AP Images)

negotiator, "is rarely able to gain at the conference table that which cannot be gained or held on the battlefield."[8]

Still, U.S. officials were pessimistic about the future. Some resigned themselves to a communist takeover of all Indochina. But Dulles and many others insisted that the United States must try, despite the odds, to hold the line at the seventeenth parallel. The "important thing," Dulles wrote, was "not to mourn the past but to seize the future opportunity to prevent the loss of northern Vietnam from leading to the extension of communism throughout Southeast Asia and the Southwest Pacific."[9] As it became clear that partition of Vietnam was the best Washington could hope for, Dulles intensified his efforts to set up an international alliance to keep Laos, Cambodia, and the southern part of Vietnam out of communist hands. His efforts came to fruition in September 1954, when the United States, Britain, France, Australia, and New Zealand joined three Asian nations—Thailand, the Philippines, and Pakistan—to form the Southeast Asia Treaty Organization (SEATO). The arrangement had obvious weaknesses, particularly the unwillingness of India, Indonesia, and other neutralist Asian nations to join. As a result, the pact inevitably had the whiff of Western domination. Another problem was the absence of Laos, Cambodia, and southern Vietnam, which were barred by the Geneva Accords from joining alliances. Still, Washington hoped SEATO would deter the communists from trying to grab more of Southeast Asia.

At the same time, the Eisenhower administration began considering how it might head off a communist takeover of southern Vietnam by converting the area into a Western-oriented bastion. Fueling U.S. hope was a provision of the Geneva deal that Americans had sought for years: the formal abolition of French rule. Although U.S. officials expected that France would continue to wield significant influence in Vietnam, they drew confidence from the prospect that Western efforts to fight communism in the region would no longer be tainted by colonialism. The path was clear to undertake a task for which Americans believed themselves, as heirs to the U.S. anticolonial tradition, uniquely qualified: to build a new anticommunist political order that would command genuine support among the Vietnamese people.

BUILDING NATIONS

The Geneva settlement faced bleak prospects from the moment it was signed. American determination to build a distinctly anticommunist state in southern Vietnam flew in the face of provisions for the reunification of the country in 1956. Meanwhile, DRV supporters, especially in the south, seethed with frustration over arrangements that fell short of their long-standing desire for national unity. Though their side had suffered more than half a million casualties during the war against France, many pledged to renew the fight at a later date. "We promise our beloved compatriots that one bright and happy day we will return," vowed one Viet Minh officer as his unit from the Mekong Delta prepared to march north, as required by the accords.[10] Perhaps most threatening of all to the peace, thousands of southerners who had fought for the Viet Minh remained below the seventeenth parallel, hostile to the Western-oriented administration there.

Nevertheless, a tenuous peace settled across Vietnam in the second half of 1954. More than one hundred thirty thousand troops under French command withdrew to the south, while about ninety thousand Viet Minh soldiers moved in the opposite direction. Both Vietnamese governments claimed to rule the entire country, but in practice both were content to set aside their conflict. For the time being, the two regimes, worn out by war and facing enormous problems within the zones they controlled, focused on consolidating their authority on either side of the seventeenth parallel—on building nations that soon came to be known around the world as North and South Vietnam.

In the North, the DRV government confronted a crippling economic crisis. Intense fighting in the Red River Delta during the closing stages of the war had devastated rice production. Traditionally, northern Vietnam had relied on food from the more productive south to make up for local shortfalls. But after the Geneva agreement, the government in Saigon blocked economic exchange between the two zones. Famine soon loomed in the North. Compounding this problem, fear of communism led many urban professionals, middle-class entrepreneurs, and Catholics—economically crucial groups—to flee to the South. Industrial activity ground almost to a standstill.

Desperate for breathing space to address these problems, the Hanoi government declared its determination to abide by the plan for peaceful reunification laid out in the Geneva Accords. Meanwhile, the government groped for solutions to its economic crisis. At times, it sought stability through moderation. Hanoi attempted to reassure segments of the population that had often backed the French—landowners, the urban middle class, and Catholics—by proclaiming its respect for private property and religious freedom. Mostly, though, the regime pursued more radical approaches. Doctrinaire communists eager to establish a socialist society accelerated an ambitious land-reform plan begun in 1953 to alleviate food shortages and break the power of the old landed elite. The effort succeeded in vastly increasing food production, but it did so at a horrific cost. Inspired by Chinese advisers who saw land reform as a vehicle for "class war," radicals persecuted not only rich landlords but also many peasants, including some who had loyally supported the Viet Minh. As many as fifteen thousand people were executed. In late 1956, widespread protests drove Ho Chi Minh to apologize for "mistakes and shortcomings" and to shake up party leadership.[11] The land reform severely heightened tensions in the countryside and led to a bloody military crackdown against dissidents in the coastal province of Nghe An.

None of this turmoil, however, seriously undermined the authority of the communist dictatorship in Hanoi. The regime solidified its position through repressive techniques including imprisonment, executions, control over the press, a crackdown on dissent among intellectuals, and heavy-handed indoctrination programs. But it also benefited from the popularity of Ho Chi Minh, more than ever the embodiment of Vietnamese nationalism, and from the efficient administrative apparatus and robust military that the DRV had developed during the long struggle against France. It is even possible that the regime's early problems helped solidify its grip on power over the long run. The land reform, for all its violence, distributed land to more than half of all North Vietnamese families, and the departure of many Catholics and much of the middle class—an exodus ultimately totaling almost a million—removed many potential opponents above the seventeenth parallel.

Basic political stability and unity in the North contrasted sharply with the situation in the South. Bao Dai's State of Vietnam confronted the task of consolidating power in a profoundly fragmented society that barely recognized central authority. Armed religious sects dominated the Mekong Delta, and a crime syndicate controlled much of Saigon. The French army continued to wield considerable power throughout the South, while Viet Minh influence lingered quietly. Making matters worse, the Bao Dai government had few tools with which to exert its authority. Thanks to years of effort by the French government to constrain Vietnamese independence, Bao Dai's regime lacked experienced administrators and possessed only a shell of an army.

On this wobbly foundation, U.S. leaders set out to build a sturdy anticommunist state. They pinned their hopes above all on

Ngo Dinh Diem, a veteran nationalist appointed prime minister by Bao Dai in June 1954. Almost alone among prominent Vietnamese politicians, Diem possessed the combination of traits that Washington hoped to foster in the new state. The son of an imperial official who had been dismissed from his job because of anticolonial views, Diem was an ardent foe of French rule. Yet he was vehemently anticommunist at the same time and had long opposed the Viet Minh. Americans were also drawn to Diem because he was a devout Catholic. Diem's religion put him in a small minority in heavily Buddhist Vietnam but held strong appeal in the United States, where the conservative political climate of the 1950s often equated Christianity with robust anticommunism.

To be sure, some U.S. officials were deeply skeptical of Diem, criticizing him as a hopelessly austere and arrogant religious zealot with little understanding of the problems confronting the vast majority of his people. "Diem impresses one as a mystic who has just emerged from a religious retreat into the cold world," wrote Douglas Dillon, the U.S. ambassador in Paris. If Diem appeared a fit candidate to lead Vietnam, Dillon warned, it was "only because the standard set by his predecessors is so low."[12] Even as Washington began backing Diem with economic and military aid, some U.S. officials championed other Vietnamese leaders for the premiership, and the Eisenhower administration came close to dropping him in 1955.

Yet for the most part the administration tolerated Diem's deficiencies, hopeful that a steady diet of American assistance would enable him to create a viable South Vietnam. Washington aimed to bolster Diem in part by damaging North Vietnam. Under the direction of Colonel Edward G. Lansdale, a team of Central Intelligence Agency operatives organized sabotage missions across the seventeenth parallel. Clandestine groups contaminated fuel supplies, destroyed printing presses, and distributed leaflets designed to scare the Northern population. They

President Dwight D. Eisenhower, standing in front of Secretary of State John Foster Dulles, welcomes South Vietnamese President Ngo Dinh Diem to Washington on May 8, 1957. (Dwight D. Eisenhower Presidential Library)

worked especially hard to encourage the exodus of refugees by spreading rumors that Catholics faced persecution and even death if they stayed in the North. The United States then provided ships for a refugee flotilla that American propagandists heralded as the "Passage to Freedom."

Meanwhile, Americans helped Diem overcome challenges to his rule in the South. At first these efforts were defensive. U.S. officials protected Diem from French hostility and from coup plots by rivals in the South Vietnamese army. In 1955, however, Americans helped Diem take the offensive. The prime minister surprised even his strongest U.S. backers by deftly using his army to defeat the criminal network that dominated Saigon and subordinating the religious sects that controlled much of the Mekong Delta. He then skillfully removed another obstacle to his authority, Bao Dai, who remained titular head of state. Diem proposed transforming South Vietnam into a republic with himself as president and called a national referendum to settle the question. He left nothing to chance, rigging the vote to win 98.2 percent of the ballots. Thus did Bao Dai's State of Vietnam come to an ignominious end. The new nation was known as the Republic of Vietnam, but it more closely resembled a dictatorship—albeit a more chaotic and permissive one than in the North—with Diem and a coterie of family members in control.

Two other threats to Diem dropped away in 1955 and 1956. First, the French government, bitter about American moves to displace it as the chief Western influence in South Vietnam, withdrew its army. That move ended lingering French hopes to oust Diem and install a more Francophile alternative, while clearing the way for an even tighter Washington-Saigon partnership. Second, Diem eliminated any possibility that the all-Vietnam elections stipulated by the Geneva Accords would be held. The Eisenhower administration was determined to avoid a vote, but wariness about seeming to violate democratic principles led it to pay lip service to the idea. The Diem government had no such qualms and bluntly rebuffed Hanoi's requests that North and South discuss procedures for the elections. The fate of the vote was sealed when the British and Soviet governments, which as chairs of the Geneva conference bore formal responsibility for enforcing the agreement, failed to back Hanoi. Both valued smooth relations with the United States far more than faithful implementation of the Geneva Accords.

Diem's string of successes generated a surge of optimism in the United States. By 1957, many Americans viewed South Vietnam, so tenuous at first, as a remarkable success story. Massachusetts senator John F. Kennedy proclaimed the country "the cornerstone of the Free World in Southeast Asia."[13] Eisenhower's rhetoric soared to similar heights as he welcomed Diem on a triumphant visit to the United States in May 1957. The South Vietnamese leader, Eisenhower declared, had "become an example for people everywhere who hate tyranny and love freedom."[14] *Life* magazine dubbed Diem "The Tough Miracle Man of Vietnam."[15]

This outpouring of adulation for Diem betrayed persistent American anxiety during the 1950s that the United States faced grave challenges in resisting communism not just in Vietnam but throughout the decolonizing world. Unquestionably, most Americans believed that the key to quick advancement for newly independent nations lay in embracing Western political and economic practices. But they also worried that the communist powers were winning the competition for influence in the Third World by using coercion and force with greater ruthlessness and by selling their ideas more persuasively. The question of how to keep emerging nations on course for Western-style "modernization" sparked intense discussion among economists and political theorists working in universities and government agencies. It also generated so much interest among the broader public that in 1958 *The Ugly American,* a collection of linked stories and vignettes purporting to instruct Americans on policymaking toward underdeveloped countries like Vietnam, became a runaway best-seller and sparked Eisenhower to appoint a committee to study how to improve U.S. aid programs overseas.[16]

By some measures, Americans were correct in viewing South Vietnam as a notable success story. Diem had undeniably overcome long odds in consolidating his rule and had performed far better than most Americans had expected. Economically, U.S. aid had enabled South Vietnam not only to survive its early trials but also to achieve a degree of prosperity. Saigon shops were well stocked with Western consumer goods, and the countryside recovered from wartime damage. "There was rice in the fields, fruit in the orchards, produce in the gardens, poultry and pigs around the house, and fish in the pond," one peasant recalled of the years after 1954.[17] Moreover, U.S. and South Vietnamese officials established reasonably smooth relations in a wide range of areas. By the late 1950s, more than fifteen hundred American specialists advised the South Vietnamese on everything from farming methods to traffic direction. Washington's bustling mission in Saigon was its largest in the world, and American aid to South Vietnam—more than $1 billion between 1955 and 1961—made Diem's tiny nation the fifth largest recipient of U.S. foreign assistance.

Behind this façade of progress and partnership, however, problems mounted. For one thing, American assistance did little to promote a healthy South Vietnamese economy for the long term. South Vietnam used U.S. aid not so much to import industrial machinery and raw materials—the kinds of goods that might have helped lay the groundwork for sustained economic development—as to acquire consumer items such as refrigerators and motorbikes. The result was an aura of middle-class prosperity in the cities but also a dangerous dependence on the United States to maintain a standard of living wildly out of line with South Vietnam's actual productive capacity.

Appearances were also deceptive in the military arena. On the positive side, Washington reorganized and reequipped the rickety force left over from the 1946–1954 war. By the late 1950s, the new Army of the Republic of Vietnam (ARVN) possessed up-to-date weaponry, numerous training centers, and auxiliary units to help with internal security. The revamped force suffered, however, from chronically poor leadership, not least because Diem, who prized loyalty over effectiveness, frequently reassigned commanders who showed initiative and skill. Many officers, meanwhile, used their posts to enrich themselves through black-marketeering, graft, and other forms of corruption.

Most problematic of all, Diem's consolidation of authority masked his failure to win support in the countryside. U.S. officials repeatedly pressed the Saigon government for land redistribution to resolve inequities left over from the French period. Diem responded with a series of halfhearted initiatives focused more on lowering rents and resettling peasants to underdeveloped areas than on reapportioning land already under cultivation. By the end of Diem's rule, only about 10 percent of more than a million tenant households in South Vietnam had obtained land, generally at high prices.[18] If Diem's land measures did nothing to improve the regime's standing, its popularity sank appreciably as a result of another initiative. In an effort to consolidate central control, Diem quashed the traditional system of local governance and appointed officials to administer South Vietnam's villages and provinces. Corruption flourished among the new appointees, chosen for their fidelity to Diem rather than their knowledge of local conditions. Burgeoning discontent with Diem's regime created fertile ground for new communist activism.

A NEW INSURGENCY

For a time, Diem coped successfully with Viet Minh supporters who had remained in the South following partition—yet another prong of his strikingly effective effort to eliminate challengers to his government. Under the slogan "Denounce the Communists," Diem moved boldly in the summer of 1955 to rout out revolutionaries. Over the next few years, the South Vietnamese army and police arrested some twenty-five thousand suspected subversives and sent them to detention camps, where many were tortured and executed.

These efforts devastated the communist movement in South Vietnam. The party lost 90 percent of its cadres and members in the South from 1955 to 1958, according to a North Vietnamese government study, and saw much of its following disintegrate.[19] "The population no longer dared to provide support, families no longer dared to communicate with their relatives in the movement, and village chapters which previously had one or two hundred members were now reduced to five or ten who had to flee into the jungle," one communist activist recalled of the mid-1950s.[20] No relief came from the North. Hanoi clung to its policy of pursuing reunification through peaceful means and discouraged its Southern comrades from fighting back against Diem's repression. That attitude reflected the belief that construction of socialism in the North must take priority over reunification as well as fears of antagonizing the communist superpowers. In 1956, the new Soviet leader, Nikita Khrushchev, proclaimed a policy of "peaceful coexistence" with the West. On a trip to Hanoi in April 1956, Soviet Politburo member Anastas Mikoyan spelled out the implications for Vietnam: Hanoi must avoid any return to war. So averse was Moscow to new international tensions over Vietnam that in 1957 it even broached the possibility of membership in the United Nations for both North and South, a move that implied the Soviet Union had given up altogether on Vietnamese reunification.

North Vietnamese leaders could not, however, ignore the increasingly desperate appeals of their Southern comrades. With the party in danger of eradication below the seventeenth parallel, leaders championing a more aggressive policy in the South gained influence. Of particular importance was Le Duan, a former political prisoner of the French who had helped lead the Viet Minh war effort in the South before becoming a key communist leader in Hanoi. In response to Le Duan's pleas to save the Southern movement, the communist party affirmed in June 1956 that the reunification struggle must remain primarily political but also endorsed armed self-defense under certain conditions. Meanwhile, party leaders declared it "extremely important" to consolidate and expand revolutionary forces in the South to prepare for the possibility of new fighting.[21] Hanoi further loosened the reins in December, authorizing Southerners to establish secret bases in remote areas and to assassinate South Vietnamese officials.

Violence steadily mounted as Southern activists responded to the changing attitude in Hanoi. In 1957 and 1958, communist fighters launched small-scale raids against government strongholds. Under the slogan "Extermination of Traitors," they also accelerated their assassination campaign, targeting especially those South Vietnamese officials who damaged the communist cause by performing their duties most capably.[22]

Yet this surge of violence reflected only an incremental change in communist policy, not a clear-cut decision to wage a new war. Hanoi leaders dubbed by historians the "North-first" faction remained convinced of the need to go slow in order to focus on internal priorities and to avoid provoking their country's foreign patrons. The key turning point came in January 1959, when communist leaders gathered once again to consider how to proceed in the South. Two developments pushed the divided party toward the more aggressive policy advocated by the "South-first" faction. First, concerns about international opposition eased as China and the Soviet Union showed greater tolerance for renewed fighting. Second, Hanoi leaders believed that Diem's policies in the countryside, while shockingly effective in destroying the communist political apparatus, had alienated much of the rural population, making peasants more likely than ever to back the communist cause. Although party leaders agreed that political organizing remained crucial to the revolutionary effort in the South, they declared in their final resolution that the "fundamental path of development for the revolution in South Vietnam is that of violent struggle."[23]

To support new military efforts in the South, Hanoi decided to build a network of trails that could be used to send troops and equipment across the seventeenth parallel. By the end of 1959, several thousand soldiers—mainly Southerners who had relocated to North Vietnam after the Geneva Accords—had crossed into the South with thirty-one tons of weapons and other supplies, the first trickle of what would become a flood of infiltration down the Ho Chi Minh Trail.[24] The communists also established a maritime infiltration route that proved crucial to supplying communist forces in the southernmost parts of South Vietnam.

The tide of events in the South began to run in favor of the communists for the first time since 1954. Even before help arrived from the North, Southern insurgents, straining against the limits imposed by Hanoi, reestablished old communist strongholds and mounted uprisings against the Saigon government in the central province of Quang Ngai and the village of Ben Tre in the Mekong Delta. As word of Hanoi's more permissive attitude spread, heartened communists staged still bolder attacks against government installations and even struck units of the South Vietnamese army. Assassinations of government officials climbed to more than one hundred and fifty per month in the first half of 1960.[25]

The final step in the North Vietnamese government's gradual shift toward war came at another landmark party meeting in September 1960. Communist leaders showed their changing attitude above all by calling for the establishment of a political organization to challenge Diem for control in South Vietnam. As so often in the past, the party opted to submerge its communist agenda within a broad coalition. On December 20, 1960, about fifty representatives of various political, religious, and ethnic groups hostile to Diem gathered at a remote spot near the Cambodian border to found the National Liberation Front. Modeled on the Viet Minh, the new group emphasized nationalist goals rather than social revolution. In this way, the organization hoped to attract a broad following and, as much as possible, to avoid provoking the United States.

By the start of 1961, then, the communists had laid the political and military groundwork for a new war. The conflict had also acquired one of the most distinct features it would have over the years to come: it was simultaneously a civil war among Southerners and a cross-border effort by Hanoi to reunify the country on its own terms, a complexity that would often elude American policymakers prone to see the conflict simply as a result of Northern aggression against the South. Unquestionably, the Second Indochina War—the conflict that would ultimately involve half a million American troops—sprang partly from efforts by the Hanoi government to control developments in the South and bring about unification under communist rule. But it also resulted from Diem's repression of a revolutionary movement that remained wedded to the vision of independence and social renovation that had underpinned the Viet Minh struggle in earlier years.

As the insurgency expanded, the South Vietnamese government lost its earlier effectiveness in dealing with the communist challenge. In fact, new efforts to fight the insurgency boomeranged spectacularly. In 1959, Saigon authorities began relocating many peasants to "agrovilles," fortified villages designed to isolate the rural population from the movement derisively labeled the "Vietcong," a contraction of the term for "Vietnamese communist." That measure alienated many peasants by requiring them to leave their ancestral homes and forcing them to endure harsh working conditions. Around the same time, Saigon enacted the even more counterproductive Decree 10/59, which classified all opposition to the government as treason and gave security forces broad authority to arrest, try, and execute suspected subversives. The behavior of the corrupt and arbitrary officials who ran the program drove many peasants into the communist fold. "The people became more angry and, as a consequence, many volunteered to join us," recalled one communist organizer.[26]

American officials watched with dread as the Saigon government faltered in the face of the growing insurgency. The news kept getting worse. Guerrilla attacks grew bolder and more destructive. American and South Vietnamese confidence in Diem's leadership plummeted. In April 1960, a group of noncommunist politicians, including some who had served in Diem's cabinet, met at the Caravelle Hotel in Saigon and issued the "Caravelle Manifesto," a declaration bitingly critical of the government. Unpopular with both peasants and urbanites, Diem's government was "in quite serious danger," Elbridge Durbrow, the U.S. ambassador in Saigon, reported to Washington in September.[27] That prognosis was affirmed two months later, when Diem barely managed to put down a coup attempt by South Vietnamese army officers upset by his management of the anticommunist fight. Whether he could survive another such challenge remained to be seen. In Washington, the problem of bolstering an increasingly precarious South Vietnam fell to President John F. Kennedy, who took office in January 1961.

ESCALATION

THE NEW KENNEDY ADMINISTRATION HAD NO ILLUSIONS
about the difficulties faced in South Vietnam. A state of "active
guerrilla warfare" existed throughout the country and the
Saigon government was nearing "the decisive phase in its battle
for survival," a U.S. government study asserted in spring 1961.[1]
The crisis only worsened over the next few years, leading some
frustrated U.S. officials—along with many journalists, members
of Congress, and leaders of allied nations—to caution against
deeper involvement. The task of stabilizing South Vietnam was,
the skeptics insisted, simply not worth the vast expenditure of
resources and blood that it seemed likely to require. A few warned
that success might not be possible at all.

In Hanoi, many North Vietnamese leaders were also wary of a
major war. They warned that further intensification of military
activity in the South risked sparking an all-out American intervention to shore up the Saigon regime. For such a small, technologically unsophisticated country as North Vietnam, it was a
fearsome prospect.

Yet in Hanoi, as in Washington, the logic of escalation prevailed. Step by step, both sides expanded their commitments to

South Vietnam between 1961 and 1965, the critical years of decision making that culminated in the dispatch of American combat forces. President Kennedy and his successor, Lyndon Johnson, followed this course not because they were confident of victory but because they feared the consequences of defeat. They worried that a communist victory would damage American interests around the world and cripple their presidencies by sparking a conservative rebellion against the Democratic Party. Meanwhile, the dominant faction of North Vietnamese policymakers calculated that intensification of the war might enable the National Liberation Front to win quickly, before the United States could bring its full military power to bear.

JFK AND VIETNAM

John F. Kennedy won the presidency largely on the strength of bold promises to wage the Cold War more vigorously than had his predecessor. "Let every nation know, whether it wishes us well or ill," Kennedy declared at his inauguration, "that we shall pay any price, bear any burden, meet any hardship, support any friend, oppose any foe, to assure the survival and the success of liberty."[2] The administration was especially eager to play an active role in the Third World. The crumbling of European empires seemed to create opportunities for spreading American influence but also to generate grave dangers that newly independent countries, anxious to end Western domination, might lean toward the communist powers. Soviet leader Nikita Khrushchev heightened American fears in January 1961 by declaring his readiness to support what he called "wars of national liberation." To combat communist insurgencies, Kennedy insisted on building up U.S. capabilities to fight small, "brushfire" wars, including the one in Vietnam.

In his bid to inject dynamism into U.S. foreign policy, Kennedy relied on a team of remarkably accomplished advisers. For secretary of defense, Kennedy chose Robert McNamara, president of Ford Motor Company and previously a professor at the Harvard Business School. Dean Rusk, a Rhodes Scholar who had worked in the State Department during the early Cold War, left the presidency of the Rockefeller Foundation to become secretary of state. McGeorge Bundy, the forty-one-year-old dean of faculty at Harvard, went to the White House as Kennedy's national security adviser, and one of the nation's foremost economists, Walt W. Rostow, became Bundy's deputy.

Ambitious and self-confident, these men believed that they could use America's vast material power to guide the development of Third World countries. They backed sharply increased spending on foreign aid and founded the Peace Corps to undertake assistance projects. At the same time, they called for a huge buildup of U.S. military capabilities. During the 1950s, they believed, American military doctrine had concentrated too heavily on nuclear arms, leaving the United States ill-equipped to fight small, low-technology wars of the sort they expected in Asia, Latin America, and Africa. Under the banner of "Flexible Response," the Kennedy team expanded American preparedness for every type of conflict. Behind this effort lay an assumption that would prove crucial to the escalation of American involvement in Vietnam over the following years: the United States could draw from this range of options to achieve precise results and could wage "limited" wars without risking nuclear Armageddon.

The most urgent crisis that Kennedy and his advisers confronted in Southeast Asia during their first months in office occurred not in Vietnam but in Laos. Just as in South Vietnam, the United States had pumped vast resources into the country since 1954 to help establish a pro-Western government. At the start of 1961, the Laotian regime faced imminent defeat by a communist movement known as the Pathet Lao. At a meeting with Kennedy the day before his inauguration, Eisenhower described the situation in stark terms. Laos was the "key to the entire area of Southeast Asia," he insisted. If Laos fell to communism, then South Vietnam, Cambodia, Thailand, and Burma would quickly follow.[3] The only solution was to send American troops, Eisenhower advised.

Kennedy's bold commitment to fight communism suggested that he would do as his predecessor proposed, and many administration officials, confident of their ability to wage limited war, urged military intervention. But the president balked. Kennedy questioned whether Laos was worth American blood and whether U.S. forces could fight effectively in such a rugged and remote country. At the end of April 1961, he announced that the United States would participate in an international conference to seek a settlement among the communist, pro-Western, and neutralist groups vying for control in Laos. More than a year of talks led to a deal in July 1962 to "neutralize" the country by setting up a coalition government and strictly limiting foreign involvement.

Although the agreement won praise around the world as a rare instance of East–West compromise, there was little chance that it would lead to lasting settlement for Laos, much less for Indochina as a whole. Like the 1954 Geneva Accords, the deal allowed the great powers to back away from an increasingly dangerous confrontation but did nothing to resolve underlying tensions. Laos remained divided among hostile factions determined to carry on their struggle for power. Moreover, the key signatories to the agreement continued to support their Laotian allies. The Kennedy administration viewed the deal as a way to carry on the fight without resorting to all-out intervention. For their part, the Soviet Union, China, and North Vietnam—the Pathet Lao's key supporters—regarded the settlement as a temporary expedient that would lessen the chance of direct American intervention and buy time for the Laotian communists to build their strength. Le Duan, elevated in 1960 to the top post in the Vietnamese communist party, appears to have hoped that the deal might also help convince U.S. leaders to negotiate a similar arrangement for Vietnam. In that way, he believed, Vietnamese communists might achieve all their objectives in the South without risking a major war against the United States.[4]

But American willingness to compromise with communists in Laos did not carry over to Vietnam. On the contrary, the administration's conciliation only heightened its determination to back the Diem regime, which appeared more than ever the cornerstone of Western influence in Southeast Asia. The administration also felt political pressure to make a stand in Vietnam. By compromising over Laos, Kennedy exposed himself to charges of appeasing communists—a line of attack with the potential to harm both Kennedy's presidency and the Democratic Party more generally. Although anticommunist fervor had ebbed since the 1950s, political leaders remembered well the hazards of appearing soft on communism. Kennedy was particularly sensitive to questions about his leadership following an embarrassing setback in Cuba. In April 1961, Cuban exiles organized by the Central Intelligence Agency were defeated in their attempt to overthrow the communist-leaning regime of Fidel Castro. Having failed in Cuba and backed down in Laos, Kennedy believed he needed to demonstrate determination. "There are just so many concessions that one can make to communists in one year and survive politically," he warned. "We just can't have another defeat this year in Vietnam."[5]

To strengthen South Vietnam, Kennedy authorized a huge expansion of American support for Ngo Dinh Diem's government. The surge began modestly in the spring of 1961, when Kennedy approved proposals to enlarge the South Vietnamese army and to send additional U.S. military advisers. Far more dramatic steps ensued several months later following an inspection tour of the area by Deputy National Security Adviser Rostow and Kennedy's top military aide, General Maxwell Taylor. Worried by the rapidly deteriorating situation they found, Rostow and Taylor advised Washington to provide far more assistance for the Diem regime, including helicopters to enable the South Vietnamese army to respond quickly to communist attacks. Still more ambitiously, they proposed dispatching eight thousand American ground soldiers to shore up the South Vietnamese war effort. To avoid alarming the communist powers, they suggested, Washington could claim it was sending troops merely to help repair damage from flooding in the Mekong Delta.

Kennedy rejected the proposal to send troops. More than most of his advisers, he feared sending Americans into combat in a distant country alongside an unpopular government facing a highly motivated adversary. He also grasped that it might prove impossible to limit the deployment once American troops began fighting and dying in significant numbers. The Joint Chiefs of Staff left no doubt as to the kind of war they had in mind, calling on the administration to send as many as two hundred thousand troops to Vietnam. Would the American public back such a commitment? Would a full-scale war be worth the diversion of American resources from elsewhere in the world? Kennedy was uncertain.

The president showed little doubt, however, about the need to support Saigon short of dispatching combat troops. Going well beyond Rostow and Taylor's aid proposals, he endorsed a massive acceleration of American involvement dubbed "Project Beefup." Military assistance more than doubled from 1961 to 1962. Meanwhile, the number of American military advisers soared from 3,205 in December 1961 to more than nine thousand a year later, and Washington established an enlarged military bureaucracy in Saigon, a body known as Military Assistance Command, Vietnam

(MACV). Kennedy also approved use of defoliants, herbicides, and napalm against communist fighters and secretly permitted U.S. advisers to take a more active role in the fighting. Americans accompanied South Vietnamese troops on combat missions, while U.S. helicopter crews ferried them in and out of battle zones.

A few U.S. officials opposed these moves, warning that South Vietnam was a hopeless cause and urging Kennedy to seek a negotiated settlement. But the president ruled out any turn to the conference table. Alongside the old geostrategic and political imperatives pushing the administration to keep up the fight, a new calculation took hold during the Kennedy years. If the United States failed to stand behind South Vietnam, officials believed, governments worldwide would doubt the credibility of American commitments. Allies would lose confidence in America's dedication to its treaty obligations, and enemies would be emboldened to foment insurgencies elsewhere. The fight in Vietnam thus seemed intertwined with American interests all over the globe.

The Kennedy administration breathed a sigh of relief during 1962, when the American buildup seemed to yield positive results, apparently vindicating the president's judgment that South Vietnam could survive without U.S. combat soldiers. Using helicopters and armored vehicles supplied by Washington, South Vietnamese forces beat back NLF attacks with new vigor. Americans also drew encouragement from a new initiative by the Diem regime to isolate the rural population from communist activists. Under the Strategic Hamlets program, the South Vietnamese government began constructing fortified settlements designed to enable local authorities to tighten control over political activity among the peasantry and to resist communist attacks more effectively. More than six hundred such hamlets, ringed by moats and bamboo spikes, were complete by the end of 1962, with hundreds more under construction.[6]

Cheered by the news from Vietnam, Kennedy instructed McNamara in July 1962 to begin planning for a gradual withdrawal of American advisers starting at the end of 1963. He did so out of confidence that the United States was achieving its goal to preserve a stable South Vietnamese state, not, as some historians have speculated, out of a desire to cut American losses in a place where the United States faced an impossible task. Indeed, when the war turned against South Vietnam in 1963, Kennedy stepped up U.S. military involvement to unprecedented levels.

THE OVERTHROW OF DIEM

Behind the veneer of progress during 1962, Diem's problems were mounting. The Strategic Hamlets program, though deeply worrying to the communists, had the unintended consequence of alienating many peasants from the Saigon government by uprooting them from their ancestral homes and failing to provide promised material benefits. Meanwhile, communists continued to win support by skillfully exploiting local grievances, especially the all-important land issue, and expanding their administrative apparatus. Even in the military arena, the South Vietnamese offensive failed to weaken the National Liberation Front in any lasting way. Communist forces remained hidden in remote locations and managed to avoid serious defeats. Indeed, communist strength increased thanks to infiltration via both overland and maritime routes. During 1962, Hanoi sent almost ten thousand fighters and, for the first time, heavy artillery down the Ho Chi Minh Trail, which the communists expanded into an elaborate network of roads running through eastern Laos.[7] At the same time, communist commanders developed methods to defeat the new helicopter-borne assaults that had put them on the defensive.

The bubble of South Vietnamese and American optimism burst in the first days of January 1963, when NLF fighters won a stunning victory near the village of Ap Bac in the Mekong Delta. South Vietnamese forces greatly outnumbered the communists and possessed vastly superior weaponry, including armored vehicles and helicopters piloted by Americans. Yet the South Vietnamese crumbled under enemy fire. The battle revealed South Vietnamese incompetence as well as new determination among communist troops to stand and fight in the face of abundant U.S.-supplied equipment. The battle showed the "coming of age" of NLF forces, asserted communist party First Secretary Le Duan.[8] But the most important outcome of the battle, described in the American press as a major defeat indicative of deep problems in South Vietnam, was to kindle new doubts in the United States about the Diem regime.

A U.S. helicopter crew chief watches ground movements during the Battle of Ap Bac on January 2, 1963. (AP Images)

Doubt turned into alarm a few months later. American officials watched with horror as Diem, abetted by his increasingly
influential brother, Ngo Dinh Nhu, cracked down on Buddhists
agitating for political reform. Tensions had simmered for years
between the Buddhist clergy and the Diem government, which
scorned Buddhists and granted privileges to Catholics. Outright
conflict began in Hue on May 8, 1963, when government troops
fired on demonstrators demanding the right to display Buddhist
prayer flags. Several activists and bystanders were killed. Protest
leaders demanded that the government end its "arrests and ter-
rorization" of Buddhists and declare religious equality.[9] But Ngo
Dinh Nhu, who spearheaded the anti-Buddhist campaign, refused to make any concessions. The crisis deepened on June 11,
when an elderly Buddhist monk dramatized his cause by burning
himself to death—a solemn gesture of defiance among Buddhists—in a Saigon intersection. A vicious cycle of confrontation
swirled during the following weeks. Buddhist demands became a
rallying point for all South Vietnamese who opposed Diem, and
more monks immolated themselves. Diem, who blamed the dis-
turbances on the communists, sent troops to ransack pagodas,
arrested hundreds of Buddhist leaders, and declared martial law.

The deepening crisis, heavily covered by the growing foreign
press corps in Saigon, confirmed for many Americans that Diem
was a narrow-minded tyrant with little legitimacy among his own
people, the vast majority of whom identified to some degree with
Buddhism. Whereas Diem's willingness to attack his enemies had
seemed an asset back in the mid-1950s, it stood out as a serious
liability by 1963. U.S. officials desperately wanted him to knit
diverse elements of South Vietnamese society into a broad front
against the communists, but he and his brother seemed to be
causing only further fragmentation. Gruesome newspaper pho-
tos of monks burning to death shocked American readers, not
least Kennedy, and suggested that South Vietnamese society was

Thich Quang Duc, a seventy-three-year-old Buddhist monk, burns himself to death at a Saigon intersection on June 11, 1963. (AP Images/Malcolm Browne)

unraveling. American outrage mounted further when Ngo Dinh Nhu's wife, best known as Madame Nhu, mocked the self-immolations as "barbeques" and expressed delight at the prospect of more.[10]

American officials demanded that Diem make peace with the Buddhists and won grudging assurances that the repression would cease. Behind the scenes, however, Diem and Nhu increasingly resented U.S. pressure. Animosity between Washington and Saigon mounted as the crisis intensified. Nhu had already complained for months that the American presence in South Vietnam had grown too large and invasive. The Americans, he charged, were running roughshod over South Vietnamese sovereignty. So exasperated did Nhu become in the summer of 1963 that he secretly made contact with North Vietnamese leaders to explore the possibility of a settlement of North-South differences that would free Saigon of its dependence on Americans. Nhu told associates that many Hanoi leaders were nationalists more than communists and were open to a Vietnamese solution to Vietnamese problems.

Nhu was probably correct in sensing opportunities for a settlement of some sort. Confronted with an increasingly chaotic situation in the South, communist leaders pursued a dual policy during much of 1963. On the one hand, they continued to expand infiltration into the South and intensified their anti-Saigon rhetoric. To overthrow Diem, there was "no alternative but to use violence," Le Duan proclaimed in March.[11] On the other hand, communist forces made no major moves to instigate an uprising against Diem or otherwise to capitalize on the Saigon government's problems. North Vietnamese leaders most likely held back in order to test the possibilities of achieving their goals peacefully, either through a deal with Nhu or, more likely, by waiting for Diem's woes to mount to the point where the United States might become willing to withdraw on terms favorable to Hanoi. Hostile moves promised to demolish these possibilities by provoking the United States to intervene more directly in the war or to overthrow Diem and bring to power a new leadership more subservient to Washington.

While Hanoi held back, key governments around the world were undoubtedly amenable to a settlement. Soviet leaders, even more than their North Vietnamese allies, feared a major war involving the United States and quietly kept alive the possibility of talks. In the West, meanwhile, the British and French governments worried that the United States faced bleak prospects in Vietnam and would be distracted from more important parts of the world— notably Europe—if it became embroiled in a war. West European interest in negotiations peaked on August 29, 1963, when French president Charles de Gaulle called publicly for talks to neutralize Vietnam. Although he did not spell out a detailed plan, de Gaulle envisioned an agreement among the great powers to reunify Vietnam under a coalition government that would ensure neither communist nor Western domination of the country.

Whether neutralization would in fact prevent an outright communist takeover was an open question, but many champions of this scheme considered that grim possibility preferable to an even grimmer war.

The rapid deterioration in South Vietnam led many Americans to think in similar ways. Influential newspapers advocated neutralization, while some liberals in Congress suggested using Diem's brutality as a pretext for negotiating a withdrawal from South Vietnam. As before, however, appeals for talks gained no traction within the executive branch. Indeed, Kennedy's aides lashed out against Nhu's flirtations with Hanoi and de Gaulle's proposal. The administration responded to the crisis in South Vietnam not by scaling back its commitment but by seeking a more compliant leadership in Saigon. At first, Americans demanded simply that Diem drop Ngo Dinh Nhu—the focus of U.S. anger—from the government and cooperate more closely with Washington. When Diem refused, the Kennedy administration turned to a more extreme solution: a coup d'état to install entirely new leaders. That possibility emerged in late August 1963, when a group of disaffected South Vietnamese generals secretly contacted U.S. representatives to test Washington's interest in overthrowing Diem. Senior U.S. officials differed over the idea, but Kennedy authorized Henry Cabot Lodge, the U.S. ambassador in Saigon, to give the green light.

For a time, nothing happened. Coup plans unraveled as suspicion and uncertainty spread among key plotters. Given a chance to reconsider their options, American policymakers bickered angrily—a sign of mounting frustration among officials who lacked any attractive options. Some advocated pressing ahead with a coup. Others warned that removing Diem would only heighten South Vietnam's instability. The president saw both sides and avoided a firm position. By not deciding, however, Kennedy effectively left the matter to Lodge, a staunch proponent of a coup. Lodge and his

A South Vietnamese soldier poses inside the ransacked Presidential Palace in Saigon following the coup that overthrew Ngo Dinh Diem on November 1, 1963. (AP Images)

aides informed the conspirators that the United States stood ready to support them. This time, the generals were better organized. On November 1, 1963, they seized key installations in Saigon and demanded the surrender of Diem and Nhu. The brothers escaped the presidential palace through a secret passageway but were captured and, despite promises of good treatment, brutally murdered in the back of an armored vehicle. Diem's tumultuous nine-year rule was over.

NEW FACES, OLD PROBLEMS

As exultant crowds in Saigon cheered the army and tore up portraits of Diem, Lodge congratulated himself on the coup. "The prospects now are for a shorter war," he cabled to Washington, confident that the new government would press the anticommunist fight more assertively.[12] But such optimism soon evaporated as U.S. officials realized they had misjudged their co-conspirators. Although headed by military officers, the new regime reflected pervasive war weariness throughout South Vietnamese society. The junta aimed not so much to step up the war effort as to broaden the Saigon government's base of political support in order to negotiate with the NLF from a position of greater strength.

Making matters worse for Washington, Hanoi responded to the coup by sharply intensifying the war in the South. Over the previous two years, North Vietnamese and NLF leaders had generally agreed on the need to restrain communist military operations, partly out of fear of irritating Moscow but largely on the calculation that there was no point in antagonizing the United States when the Diem regime seemed likely to collapse under the weight of its own shortcomings. The coup eliminated the latter motive for caution by bringing to power a South Vietnamese government that appeared, at least initially, to enjoy the twin advantages of considerable popularity and redoubled U.S. backing. At contentious party meetings in November and December 1963, communist leaders agreed that the time had come for bolder military moves. Hanoi still showed a degree of caution, rejecting proposals to send large numbers of regular North Vietnamese troops across the seventeenth parallel. But they decided nonetheless to strengthen the Southern insurgency in hopes of scoring quick battlefield victories that would bring the NLF to power before the United States could intervene more fully.

These decisions marked a major victory for Le Duan, who had been arguing for years in favor of bold action in the South, and other militants such as Le Duc Tho and Nguyen Chi Thanh, party leaders who would become increasingly prominent in managing the war. Meanwhile, party officials who backed a more cautious policy were increasingly marginalized. The hawks, openly espousing a Maoist vision of aggressive insurgent warfare over the restrained approach preferred by Moscow, ousted many moderates from government posts and placed some under house arrest. Revealingly, even Ho Chi Minh, who had thrived for so many years through his remarkable ability to bring together revolutionaries of different political stripes, found himself on the sidelines. At more than seventy years old, the towering figure of the Vietnamese revolution became a figurehead with little authority over day-to-day policymaking.[13] The coup thus backfired on the United States, exacerbating the political problems that it faced in South Vietnam and emboldening militants in Hanoi.

Another momentous development in November 1963—the assassination of Kennedy—compounded the setback by ensuring that there would be no reappraisal of the American commitment in the months ahead. To be sure, it is doubtful that Kennedy would have taken early steps toward negotiation or withdrawal. For more than two years, after all, he had massively expanded the American investment in Vietnam. Yet Kennedy possessed a nuanced grasp of the difficulties confronting the United States in Vietnam and saw reasons to avoid introduction of combat forces. It is plausible to speculate that Washington might have pulled back from Vietnam rather than send Americans into battle if he, rather than the less subtle Lyndon Johnson, had occupied the White House in 1965, when a choice could no longer be deferred.

From the outset of his presidency, Johnson took a belligerent position on Vietnam. "We should all of us let no day go by without asking whether we are doing everything we can to win the struggle there," he told administration officials during his second week in office.[14] Johnson's attitude reflected his unwavering acceptance of the geostrategic assumptions that had underpinned American involvement in Vietnam for several years. As Senate majority leader in the 1950s and then as vice president, he had spoken apocalyptically about the risks of communist advances, warning at one point that the United States would have to "surrender the Pacific and take up our defenses on our own shores" if the communists prevailed in Southeast Asia.[15] After rising to the presidency, Johnson saw additional reasons to take a hard line. For one, he believed that at a moment of national grieving for Kennedy it was politically vital to stick with his predecessor's policies, especially in foreign affairs. Johnson lacked confidence in that arena and leaned heavily on Kennedy's key advisers.

The new president also believed that he needed to take a bold stand against communist expansion to win approval for his ambitious domestic agenda. Johnson, who had come to prominence as a champion of the New Deal during the 1930s, aspired to build on earlier liberal accomplishments by promoting civil rights, fighting poverty, improving education, and expanding health care—a raft of legislative initiatives aimed at creating what he would later proclaim the "Great Society." He knew, however, that he faced skepticism from conservatives, including southerners in his own party, and feared he would have no chance to accomplish his goals if he left himself vulnerable to criticism for weakness against communism. The furor that Joseph McCarthy had raised against Harry Truman over the "loss" of China back in the early 1950s was "chickenshit" compared with the conservative backlash he expected if the communists took South Vietnam, Johnson asserted years later.[16]

While Johnson affirmed the American commitment, the news from Vietnam kept getting worse. Following an inspection trip to South Vietnam in December 1963, Secretary of Defense McNamara reported that the insurgents controlled even more territory than American officials had feared. The Strategic Hamlet program was crumbling, and chaos reigned in the cities. If nothing was done to reverse the trend, McNamara predicted, the country would collapse within two or three months. Disappointed by the rulers it had just helped install, Washington threw its support behind another coup, this one carried out bloodlessly by General Nguyen Khanh on January 29, 1964. The Johnson administration hoped that Khanh would live up to his promises to wage the war more effectively, but the leadership change made little difference.

Within the United States and around the world, a growing chorus appealed for a negotiated settlement that would allow Washington to save face while disengaging from a hopeless situation. Key members of the Senate, along with a mounting number of editorial pages around the nation, urged Johnson to pursue any avenue that might lead to a peaceful outcome. Even within the administration, several midlevel officials urged caution. Most strikingly, David Nes, the second-ranking diplomat in Saigon, argued in a February 1964 memorandum that basic social trends in South Vietnam made an American victory impossible. "The peasants who form the mass of the South Vietnamese population are exhausted and sick of twenty years of civil conflict," Nes asserted. "On the other hand, the Viet Cong represents a grass roots movement which is disciplined, ideologically dedicated, easily identifiable with the desires of the peasantry and of course ruthless."[17] Internationally, American allies sometimes sympathized with U.S. objectives but doubted whether they could be achieved at a reasonable cost. Britain, Canada, and other Western governments rejected American appeals for help in Vietnam and quietly urged Washington to cut its losses.

Privately, Johnson confessed deep worries about Vietnam and had no enthusiasm for deepening the American commitment. "It's just the biggest damn mess that I ever saw," he lamented to a confidant in May 1964.[18] But the president and his advisers refused to consider backing down. The key question for them was not whether, but how, to prop up South Vietnam. Increasingly, they concluded that the United States, to have any hope of success in Southeast Asia, must expand its military activities. Planning focused on an old idea—the introduction of American combat troops to bolster the South Vietnamese army—and a new one: launching air attacks against North Vietnam to coerce it into ending support for the Southern insurgency. By the middle of 1964, a consensus had formed among Johnson's key advisers and the military that one or both of these moves would be necessary.

Yet Johnson was loath to take either step in the short term. He worried that the Khanh government was too frail to withstand a larger war. More important, he feared that any abrupt departures in Vietnam might hurt him in the presidential election that November. Although polls showed that he enjoyed a huge lead over his Republican challenger, Senator Barry Goldwater of Arizona, Johnson believed that a major expansion of the war might cause both liberals and centrists to have second thoughts. The trick was to display firmness on the Vietnam issue while deferring any dramatic moves until after the election.

DECISIONS FOR WAR

Keenly attuned to his electoral prospects, Johnson authorized only minor invigoration of the war effort in 1964, even as he and his advisers contemplated a major escalation later. Johnson increased the number of U.S. military advisers to 23,300 by the end of the year and appointed a new American commander, General William Westmoreland, in the hope that the veteran of the Second World War and Korea would deliver better results. In a sign of things to come, the administration also approved a plan for gradually stepping up military pressure on North Vietnam, especially by supporting South Vietnamese sabotage raids against Northern targets.

These initiatives, like so many that had preceded them, did little to strengthen South Vietnam. In only one respect—the one that mattered most to Johnson in the near term—did he find success during 1964: he managed to keep Vietnam from harming his electoral prospects. In fact, he probably enhanced his standing by demonstrating a deft blend of boldness and restraint when a crisis erupted three months before the vote. On August 2, an American destroyer, the USS *Maddox*, came under attack from North Vietnamese torpedo boats in the Gulf of Tonkin in retaliation against South Vietnamese commando raids on the Northern coast. The *Maddox*, unharmed, returned fire and sank one torpedo boat. Two nights later, the captain of another destroyer, the USS *Turner Joy*, reported on the basis of sketchy radar and sonar readings that his ship had been similarly targeted.

Some U.S. officials doubted that the second attack had actually occurred—skepticism vindicated by later investigations. But Johnson had little interest in ascertaining the facts. Rather, sensing an opportunity to mollify conservatives who had been calling for more aggressive action in Vietnam, he ordered an air strike against North Vietnamese naval installations. Johnson also exploited the episode by persuading Congress to give him the power to take further military action if he saw fit. On August 7, after minimal debate, the House and Senate overwhelmingly passed the Gulf of Tonkin Resolution, which authorized the president to take "all necessary measures" to resist aggression in Vietnam.[19] With politicians across the political spectrum eager to burnish their anticommunist credentials ahead of the November elections, even members of Congress skeptical of American commitments in Vietnam backed the measure without quibble. The only opposition came from two liberal Democrats, Senators Ernest Gruening of Alaska and Wayne Morse of Oregon.

The Gulf of Tonkin affair served Johnson's political interests in various ways. The air strike, combined with Johnson's clear affirmations of American support for South Vietnam, produced a 30-point surge in the president's approval ratings. Even better for Johnson, the episode neutralized Vietnam as a campaign issue. Once he had demonstrated his willingness to use force, the Republicans could no longer assail him for weakness. Newly invulnerable on the right, Johnson accentuated a moderate position on Vietnam over the remainder of the campaign. "We are not about to send American boys nine or ten thousand miles away from home to do what Asian boys ought to be doing for themselves," he told one audience.[20] Such assertions enhanced Johnson's standing with centrist voters who favored firmness against communism but opposed direct involvement of American troops. Partly as a result of his apparent moderation on Vietnam, Johnson won the largest presidential landslide in American history.

The conclusion of the campaign enabled Johnson and his advisers to refocus on Vietnam free of the political calculations that had constrained them for several months. The situation they confronted was more ominous than ever. The increasingly unpopular General Khanh had resigned in August, initiating a series of leadership changes. War weariness and anti-Americanism intensified dramatically over the second half of 1964. Further complicating matters for Washington, Johnson's air strike against North Vietnam, far from deterring communist activities in the South, had the opposite effect. In September, Hanoi sent units of the regular North Vietnamese army to the South for the first time. Communist leaders, viewing the bombing attacks as the likely first step in a major American escalation, hoped that increased infiltration would bring victory before the United States could intervene more decisively on behalf of Saigon. But Hanoi also braced itself for a protracted international conflict by soliciting greater aid from China and the Soviet Union. Thus did the escalatory cycle take another turn toward full-scale war involving both North Vietnamese and U.S. troops.

The situation in South Vietnam, coupled with fears that John-son's sweeping electoral victory might embolden him to step up American involvement, produced a fresh wave of appeals in late 1964 and early 1965 for the United States to pull back. From Canada to Japan, American allies refused persistent U.S. requests for help in Vietnam and warned of mounting risks. French pres-ident Charles de Gaulle renewed his neutralization proposal, in-sisting that such a scheme, though far from perfect, was better than waging an unwinnable war. Within the Johnson administration, meanwhile, no less a figure than Vice President Hubert Humphrey weighed in against escalation. In a memo to the president in mid-February 1965, Humphrey insisted that Johnson's massive elec-toral victory gave him the freedom to draw back from Vietnam without fear of political attack from conservatives. In fact, Hum-phrey prophetically advised, a major war would create a much more serious problem for Johnson—opposition from his core Democratic Party supporters.

Johnson ignored these appeals and, in a series of crucial decisions from November 1964 to March 1965, dramatically ex-panded the U.S. military role in Vietnam. Though the adminis-tration moved slowly and deliberately during these months, its caution did not reflect uncertainty about the need to expand the war. At each stage, Johnson chose from a narrow range of op-tions, all of which presupposed the necessity of fighting to pre-serve an anticommunist South Vietnam. Rather, Johnson's caution reflected three calculations that led him to eschew drastic moves. First, he feared that rapid escalation might provoke China or the Soviet Union to intervene more aggressively in Vietnam, transforming the conflict into a dangerous confrontation be-tween nuclear-armed superpowers. Second, he worried that dra-matic steps might topple the teetering South Vietnamese government by inviting communist reprisals. Third, he feared that expansion of the war would distract attention from his domestic agenda, which he had begun to implement.

The first landmark American decision came less than a month after the election. Rejecting more extreme proposals by the Joint Chiefs of Staff, Johnson approved a two-stage plan of aerial bombing. The first phase consisted of limited attacks on the Ho Chi Minh Trail in Laos as well as what American officials dubbed "tit for tat" raids against North Vietnam in response to communist attacks in the South. The second phase involved a sustained bombing campaign against North Vietnam lasting from two to six months—an operation that, Johnson understood, would require the introduction of American ground troops to guard U.S. airbases. The president immediately approved bombing against targets in Laos, but he held back from attacking North Vietnam out of fear that South Vietnam was still too weak to withstand a wider war.

With the Saigon government apparently on its last legs after another coup at the end of January, U.S. leaders faced a crucial moment of decision. "The time has come for harder choices," Bundy and McNamara advised the president. They warned that the United States was courting "disastrous defeat" by insisting that Saigon put its house in order before bombing of the North could begin.[21] Johnson agreed. "We have kept our gun over the mantle and our shells in the cupboard for a long time now," the president declared. "I can't ask our American soldiers out there to continue to fight with one hand tied behind their backs."[22] Johnson insisted only that the United States wait for a pretext to begin the campaign. It did not take long. On February 7, NLF troops attacked U.S. bases at Pleiku, killing eight Americans. In response, Johnson ordered U.S. aircraft to strike military bases in North Vietnam. Less than a month later, the administration initiated Operation Rolling Thunder, its campaign of sustained bombing against the North.

From the initiation of Rolling Thunder, it was but a short step to the introduction of U.S. combat troops. In late February 1965, General Westmoreland appealed to Washington for two battalions of Marines to guard a major U.S. airfield at Da Nang. A few American officials questioned whether U.S. troops were adequately prepared to fight a guerrilla-style war and doubted that it would be possible to limit further deployments once Americans were in combat. On the whole, though, Westmoreland's request stirred little debate among officials who had already accepted the probability of sending ground soldiers. Johnson approved Westmoreland's request, and on March 8, 1965, the Marines waded ashore near Da Nang. The United States was at war in the air and on the ground.

WAR ON MANY FRONTS

EVEN AS THE UNITED STATES WENT TO WAR, President Johnson made clear there would be no departure from the gradualism that had guided him up to that point. "I'm going up old Ho Chi Minh's leg an inch at a time," he boasted.[1] By slowly ratcheting up the scale and intensity of the American war effort, Johnson aimed to find North Vietnam's breaking point—the level of destruction and death that would lead Hanoi to sue for peace on Washington's terms. Few Americans doubted that the United States, the world's mightiest nation, could force a country as poor and weak as North Vietnam to its knees.

North Vietnamese leaders foresaw a different outcome. American troops were ill-suited to fight guerrillas in a distant, alien landscape, Le Duan, the first secretary of the Vietnamese communist party, told a meeting of top Hanoi officials in July 1965. Le Duan predicted, moreover, that the American public would have little stomach for a long war, while Vietnamese revolutionaries would absorb whatever punishment the Americans inflicted for as long as necessary. "The North will not count the cost," he declared.[2]

Le Duan's analysis proved closer to the mark. Unquestionably, American intervention, which the communists had hoped for years to avoid, posed serious problems for Hanoi and the NLF. But the communists adapted to the new situation and learned to exploit their adversaries' weaknesses, as they had for decades when facing setbacks. On the battlefield, they fought the United States to a stalemate even as American power grew rapidly between 1965 and 1968. In the political arena, the Saigon government persistently failed to gain legitimacy as the war dragged on, while the American public increasingly questioned U.S. policy.

TOWARD A MAJOR WAR

Once U.S. Marine units had disembarked in Vietnam, pressure mounted quickly on the Johnson administration to undertake a major ground war. In late March 1965, the Joint Chiefs of Staff asked for three divisions of U.S. soldiers and permission to use them in offensive operations throughout South Vietnam. The request put Johnson in a familiar bind. On the one hand, the president and his advisers accepted the military's contention that bombing by itself would accomplish little in the short run and that the Saigon regime might collapse without a major infusion of American manpower. On the other, Johnson continued to fear that drastic steps in Vietnam would imperil his domestic agenda and risk provoking a war with China. As usual, Johnson opted for the middle ground, giving the military most—but not all—that it requested. He agreed to send forty thousand new troops and to allow U.S. forces to undertake offensive operations. But he ordered that they do so only within four limited "enclaves" surrounding key bases along the coast.

Johnson also sought to minimize the risks of escalation by ensuring that these decisions, among the most momentous in the long process of deepening American involvement, attracted as little public attention as possible. The administration explained the bombing of North Vietnam simply as retaliation for communist attacks in the South and never announced the switch to sustained strikes. Similarly, administration officials downplayed the commitment of combat troops and publicly acknowledged the shift to offensive operations only in the course of a routine press briefing weeks later. Thus Johnson committed the United States to a major war without ever forthrightly saying so.

Inevitably, though, the administration faced criticism as news of the expanded commitment trickled out. Many conservatives demanded that Johnson escalate more quickly. Meanwhile, proponents of negotiation and disengagement grew more vocal as the war heated up. University professors organized "teach-ins" on Vietnam, and students staged demonstrations. On April 17, 1965, more than fifteen thousand protesters attended the first antiwar march in Washington. Internationally, Britain, Canada, and other American allies, joined by the secretary general of the United Nations and many nonaligned governments, urged negotiations more strongly than ever.

Such criticism led Johnson to speak out about the war, but he remained determined to minimize controversy. In a major speech at Johns Hopkins University on April 7, 1965, he sought to mold public opinion by appealing to critics on both sides. To mollify the hawks, Johnson reaffirmed his commitment to an independent South Vietnam. To assuage the doves, he declared his willingness to join in "unconditional discussions" for a peaceful settlement and even proposed a billion-dollar development program for Vietnam modeled on America's Tennessee Valley Authority.[3]

The speech led to a flurry of gestures by both Washington and Hanoi suggesting interest in a diplomatic solution. The day after the president's address, North Vietnamese Prime Minister Pham Van Dong laid out a four-point program for a peace settlement—U.S. withdrawal, respect for the 1954 Geneva agreements, implementation of the NLF agenda demanding elections for a new South Vietnamese government, and eventual reunification. Although he did not say so explicitly, Pham Van Dong left open the possibility that these demands constituted merely an opening bargaining position rather than preconditions for a settlement—a key distinction apparently designed to make the proposal attractive to Washington. A month later, Johnson approved a five-day pause in the bombing to indicate his openness to talks.

This maneuvering came to nothing, however, for neither government had any serious intention of negotiating. On the contrary, each saw a better chance of achieving its aims on the battlefield than at the bargaining table. Johnson and his advisers recognized that they held a weak hand because of the dismal political and military condition of South Vietnam. They insisted that talks could occur only once the situation improved dramatically—sufficiently, that is, to enable them to dictate terms to Hanoi. On the communist side, some policymakers genuinely backed negotiations. These officials worried that American bombing would cripple North Vietnam and that an expanded war would harm relations with Beijing and Moscow. But Le Duan and other hawkish leaders prevailed, as they had since at least 1963. These policymakers still hoped to topple the Saigon government quickly, before American escalation went much further. Even if that did not happen, though, they believed superior morale, patience, and tactical innovation would eventually carry them to victory over any size force the Americans chose to send. "We will fight," Le Duan boasted in May 1965, "whatever way the United States wants."[4]

Such confidence came partly from Hanoi's success in securing help from China and the Soviet Union. Soviet leaders, hoping to avoid a major war in Southeast Asia, had cut their aid to North Vietnam in 1964. But intense Sino-Soviet animosity—a major feature of the Cold War in the 1960s—led new Soviet leader Leonid Brezhnev to step up support for North Vietnam in 1965. Soviet policymakers feared that failure to do so would cede Southeast Asia to Chinese domination and weaken Soviet claims to leadership throughout the Third World. On a trip to Hanoi in February 1965, Soviet Prime Minister Alexei Kosygin pledged "all necessary support and assistance" for North Vietnam and initiated an aid program that ultimately delivered vast stocks of military supplies.[5]

For his part, Chinese leader Mao Zedong feared direct U.S.-Chinese fighting and hinted repeatedly that China would not intervene in Vietnam as long as U.S. ground forces did not invade the North. Still, eager to demonstrate his commitment to worldwide revolution, Mao responded enthusiastically to Hanoi's appeals for increased aid in early 1965. "Our principle is that we will do our best to provide you with whatever you need and whatever we have," pledged one of Mao's top lieutenants, Liu Shaoqi.[6] Starting in June, China sent huge quantities of goods—everything from munitions and food to toothpaste and recreational equipment—along with thousands of troops to repair roads and carry out other tasks. Although China never dispatched combat units, the support troops it sent, peaking at about one hundred seventy thousand in 1967, freed North Vietnamese soldiers to fight below the seventeenth parallel.

Hanoi's confidence also sprang from the rapidly evolving military and political situation in the South. Reinforced by North Vietnamese regulars, the NLF launched a major offensive in May and scored numerous victories. Despite years of U.S. aid, the Army of the Republic of Vietnam neared the brink of collapse. The same seemed to be true of the government in Saigon. In June, yet another turn of the leadership carousel brought to power a military junta led by Air Vice Marshal Nguyen Cao Ky and Army General Nguyen Van Thieu, men with virtually no political support beyond the disintegrating military sphere from which they came. The two men seemed "the bottom of the barrel, absolutely the bottom of the barrel," U.S. Assistant Secretary of Defense William Bundy remembered later.[7]

This deterioration led to the largest escalatory steps yet by the United States. More convinced than ever that South Vietnam was crumbling, U.S. commanders asked for one hundred fifty thousand more troops and permission to use them offensively throughout South Vietnam. These requests sparked a series of intense discussions among the president, his top advisers, and congressional leaders during July—the closest that Washington came to thoroughly debating whether to wage a major war. A few participants, especially Undersecretary of State George Ball, argued vigorously against the expansion, warning that the United States was poorly prepared to fight a guerrilla conflict in a remote, alien country. But the most influential policymakers, particularly McNamara and Rusk, backed the military, restating old concerns about protecting American credibility and propping up wobbly dominoes. "If the Communist world finds out we will not pursue our commitments," said Rusk, "I don't know where they will stay their hand."[8] McNamara predicted that defeat in South Vietnam would lead to communist control in Laos, Cambodia, Thailand, Burma, and probably Malaysia within three years, while governments as distant as Greece and Turkey would question their alliances with Washington.

Johnson asked probing questions and expressed anxiety about the many problems the United States faced in Vietnam. Nevertheless, at the end of July he approved a major expansion of the ground war. As before, the president did not go as far as the military asked. He ordered the immediate dispatch of fifty thousand troops, with another fifty thousand to follow before the end of the year and, very likely, still more after that. But he also approved the military's request to use U.S. forces all over South Vietnam. The way was clear for the United States to take over the main burden of the fighting.

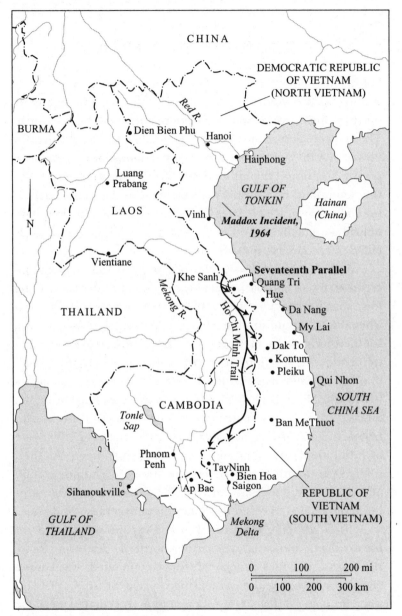

Map of Vietnam, Laos, and Cambodia showing major sites of the American war.

BOMBING THE NORTH

For the next three years, the United States struggled to achieve its goal—a secure, noncommunist South Vietnam—by simultaneously waging a ground war in the South and bombing the North. The air campaign against North Vietnam had three objectives: to bolster South Vietnamese morale by demonstrating American resolve, to prevent the infiltration of troops and equipment into the South, and to punish North Vietnam to the point where it would beg for peace on American terms. The bombing may have helped marginally to achieve the first goal, but it unquestionably failed to accomplish the other two.

As with the ground war, Johnson escalated U.S. bombing incrementally, an approach that angered military aides eager to try for a massive knockout blow. At first, U.S. attacks focused overwhelmingly on infiltration routes and military bases in the southernmost parts of North Vietnam. Those strikes wrought tremendous devastation. "The trees were completely destroyed," one North Vietnamese soldier later recalled of the approaches to Ho Chi Minh Trail in 1966. "It was like traveling through a desert."[9] Still, Hanoi managed not only to sustain the flow of troops and matériel to the South but even to increase it. The rate of infiltration rose from an average of about fifteen hundred soldiers per month in 1965 to forty-five hundred a month in 1966 and six thousand a month in 1967.[10] Only 10 to 20 percent of infiltrators failed to reach the South, usually because of disease.

Frustrated, some U.S. officials urged expansion of the target list to include industrial sites farther north. By destroying factories, ports, and fuel depots, advocates contended, the United States would reduce the war-making capacity of North Vietnam while inflicting sufficient punishment to push Hanoi to plead for negotiations. For months, Johnson resisted this pressure, hoping that the mere threat of bombing North Vietnam's industrial core would be enough to force Hanoi to back down. Johnson even halted the bombing for thirty-seven days in December 1965 and January 1966 in a bid to influence Hanoi with the promise of peace as well as the devastation wrought by U.S. firepower. North Vietnam remained defiant, however, and in June 1966, Johnson approved a drastic expansion of the bombing. Over the next three months, U.S. bombs destroyed 75 percent of North Vietnam's oil storage capacity.

The logic of further escalation proved irresistible as Hanoi held firm in the months that followed. Neither the president nor his advisers could imagine that such a weak nation—a "damn little pissant country," as Johnson put it[11]—could hold out indefinitely. It was just a matter of time, they continued to believe, before the United States would finally break Hanoi's will. In this quest, massive B-52s and other American aircraft made 79,000 bombing runs against North Vietnam in 1966, a threefold increase over the year before, and 108,000 in 1967. By the end of 1968, the United States had dropped 643,000 tons of bombs on the country and expanded its target list to include even heavily populated industrial areas close to the center of Hanoi and previously off-limits sites near the Chinese border. In all, Rolling Thunder destroyed 59 percent of North Vietnam's power plants, 55 percent of its major bridges, and almost ten thousand vehicles.[12] The bombing also killed an estimated fifty-two thousand North Vietnamese and took an enormous physical and psychological toll on many others. "I saw children who had been killed, pagodas and churches that had been destroyed, monks and priests dead in the ruins, schoolboys who were killed when schools were bombed," an engineer from Haiphong later recalled.[13]

Despite such horrors, Hanoi's breaking point remained elusive. North Vietnam's ability to persevere may have resulted in part from the way Washington managed the bombing. As critics of the Johnson administration have long charged, incremental expansion of the attacks gave North Vietnam time to disperse its modest industrial facilities and organize its population to withstand the onslaught. But the American failure resulted more fundamentally from misjudgments about the susceptibility of North Vietnam to bombing. No matter how fiercely it attacked the Ho Chi Minh Trail, the United States stood little chance of completely strangling the flow of troops and equipment to the South. North Vietnamese and NLF soldiers got most of their supplies from Southern villagers and, by one estimate early in the war, required only thirty-four tons of supplies each day from the North—a paltry amount that could be transported by just seven large trucks.[14] North Vietnam also kept supplies moving south via the sea, notably along a new infiltration route that passed through the Cambodian port of Sihanoukville. Nor were Americans correct in the belief that ravaging North Vietnamese industry would force Hanoi to buckle. Although Ho Chi Minh's government had pumped resources into industry since 1954, North Vietnam remained an overwhelmingly agricultural society with low dependence on factories, power plants, and other installations that American policymakers targeted in hope of inflicting unbearable damage.

Hanoi's stamina was also fortified by the increasing flow of Chinese and Soviet assistance. Chinese troops helped repair bomb damage, while both communist powers sent food, fuel, vehicles, diesel generators, and other goods crucial to maintaining basic economic activity in North Vietnam. Additionally, the Soviet Union provided sophisticated antiaircraft weapons and crews to operate them, giving North Vietnam the kernel of what would become the most elaborate air-defense system in the world. Although countermeasures by U.S. pilots proved generally effective, North Vietnamese defenses exacted a draining toll. The United States lost nine hundred fifty aircraft, worth a total of about $6 billion, over North Vietnam. Those losses contributed to one of the most revealing statistics of the entire war: the bombing campaign cost the

United States $6.60 for every dollar of damage it caused in the North in 1965 and $9.60 the next year.[15] Aircraft losses brought another problem as well. North Vietnam captured 356 American aviators, who, along with 209 other prisoners of war, gave Hanoi a valuable bargaining chip that it would exploit later in peace talks with Washington.

North Vietnam also withstood U.S. bombing through its own resourcefulness. The government moved factories and fuel supplies to remote locations, sometimes underground tunnels or caves, and assigned women to replace military-age men in both factory and field. Everywhere, North Vietnamese dug bomb shelters—more than twenty million over the course of the war, by Hanoi's count.[16] "Call the Shelter Your Second Home," government sloganeers proclaimed.[17] Meanwhile, Hanoi recruited hundreds of thousands of North Vietnamese, mostly young women, to repair bomb damage. Crews fixed roads, railways, and bridges throughout the country but labored especially on the infiltration routes, where American bombing was heaviest. Engineers designed pontoon bridges that could be dismantled when not in use, and truck drivers learned to camouflage their vehicles and to drive at night without headlights.

All of this was accomplished through severe regimentation of North Vietnamese society and strong doses of anti-American propaganda. The Hanoi dictatorship sponsored plays, songs, and postage stamps celebrating the shooting down of American bombers, while propagandists flooded the country with patriotic appeals and withheld information about casualties. There is little evidence, however, that Hanoi depended heavily on outright coercion of the population. In fact, North Vietnamese morale appears to have remained reasonably strong during the years of sustained American bombing. Interviewed in later years, North Vietnamese civilians remembered the bombing as a time of extreme hardship, shortages, and the ever-present danger of death. But they also recalled strong patriotism and profound disgust for their enemies as the damage mounted. "They turned their hatred into activity," one North Vietnamese villager recalled of his compatriots.[18]

THE WAR IN THE SOUTH

The war in South Vietnam followed much the same pattern as in the North. To break the communists' will, Washington repeatedly expanded its commitment. American personnel in South Vietnam totaled 184,300 at the end of 1965, 385,300 a year later, and 485,600 at the end of 1967, peaking at 543,400 in April 1969. These forces undertook increasingly ambitious operations, while U.S. aircraft pummeled communist-held areas of the South with more than one million tons of bombs between 1965 and 1968, twice the tonnage dropped on the North. Yet communist forces managed not only to withstand American escalation but even to increase their own military capabilities in the South.

From the start, the Joint Chiefs of Staff pursued a strategy of attrition. Under that approach, American commanders aimed to locate and then annihilate concentrations of enemy troops. Over time, they hoped, aggressive "search-and-destroy" operations would inflict casualties more quickly than North Vietnam and the NLF could replace their losses, thus forcing the communists to seek peace on American terms. Critics complained that the attrition strategy ignored the need to stamp out insurgent political organizing among the civilian population of South Vietnam. But Westmoreland maintained that a strategy centered on population control would require more troops than he had and would result in a longer war than the American public would tolerate. The task of building security in the countryside—"pacification," in military parlance—thus fell largely to the South Vietnamese army.

The attrition strategy depended on grueling infantry patrols to flush the enemy out of its hiding places. Fundamentally, though, search-and-destroy was designed to minimize U.S. casualties by emphasizing mobility, technology, and firepower, categories in which U.S. forces enjoyed huge advantages. To find communist units, they relied on aerial surveillance, radar, and even devices that detected the smell of human urine. Meanwhile, American planes dropped millions of gallons of Agent Orange and other chemical defoliants to prevent communist forces from maneuvering beneath Vietnam's vast jungle canopy. Once enemy units were located, U.S. forces sought to pounce on them quickly and inflict as high a "body count" as possible. Helicopters rushed soldiers to the battlefield, while aircraft and artillery pounded enemy positions.

Westmoreland achieved his most urgent objective in the early days of the U.S. intervention—to stave off the collapse of South Vietnam. By the end of 1965, U.S. forces had blunted communist momentum, giving the Saigon government a new lease on life. Westmoreland failed, however, to accomplish his next goal—to break the back of communist forces during 1966. Unquestionably, U.S. forces inflicted heavy casualties on North Vietnamese and NLF units. Roughly 179,000 communist troops were killed from 1965 to 1967, more than three times the number of deaths on the U.S.–South Vietnamese side. Yet, for a number of reasons, North Vietnam and the NLF were able to persevere and fight the Americans to a stalemate.

Most important, the communists maintained a steady flow of troops to replace casualties between 1965 and 1967. In this way, Westmoreland's attrition strategy never reached the all-important "crossover point"—the moment when NLF and North Vietnamese losses exceeded their ability to put new forces in the field. To the contrary, communist forces in the South expanded in this period, numbering perhaps half a million by 1967 (against roughly

1.3 million on the U.S.–South Vietnamese side). This growth resulted mainly from Hanoi's success in keeping North Vietnamese soldiers flowing down the Ho Chi Minh Trail despite American bombing. Behind that achievement lay a larger demographic advantage. Each year, approximately two hundred thousand North Vietnamese males reached draft age.[19]

At the same time, the NLF continued to recruit new soldiers within South Vietnam. The intensification of the war made that task much harder. Peasants throughout the South increasingly resented the communists as peace seemed to recede into the indefinite future and the party lost its aura of invincibility. More and more, remembered one villager from the Mekong Delta, peasants grew "exhausted and paralyzed in body and spirit."[20] Whereas voluntarism had once sufficed, the communists increasingly depended on taxation, forced labor, and conscription. Morale problems did not, however, seriously reduce communist troop strength. In hotly contested Long An province, for example, the size of locally raised NLF units increased from 1965 to 1966, dipped slightly in 1967, and then increased again in 1968.[21]

The perseverance of NLF and North Vietnamese forces also resulted from decisions to fight in a way that husbanded resources while exploiting American vulnerabilities. To be sure, communist commanders responded to the introduction of American combat forces in 1965 by attempting to score major battlefield victories. When that approach brought little but massive casualties, however, they pulled back to a more conservative approach that matched the American attrition strategy with an attrition strategy of their own. Under this approach, the communists aimed to maintain constant pressure on the Americans but to risk large confrontations only when they held decisive advantages. When the battlefield situation turned against them, they would withdraw to fight another day. Through a combination of large battles and guerrilla attacks, Hanoi and the NLF aimed to wear down not only American forces but also—and just as crucially—the American public. This approach required "high courage, a strong will, and great patience," warned communist General Nguyen Chi Thanh.[22] But he believed that it would ultimately pay off by leading a frustrated and bloodied United States to withdraw from Vietnam, just as France had in the 1950s.

The effectiveness of the communists' approach was reflected in the outcomes of major operations undertaken by U.S. forces. During 1966 and 1967, Westmoreland repeatedly sent large forces to destroy NLF bases near Saigon. In Operations Attleboro, Cedar Falls, and Junction City, U.S. and South Vietnamese troops killed thousands of enemy soldiers and seized tons of weapons, while razing hostile villages and wide swaths of jungle. Through it all, aircraft and artillery pulverized the area to assure that nothing remained of the communist strongholds. And yet none of these stunning displays of mobility and firepower succeeded in uprooting communist forces permanently. Each time, NLF fighters retreated into elaborate underground tunnel complexes or across the border into Cambodia, where Americans were not allowed to chase them. When U.S. and South Vietnamese forces withdrew, the communists moved back in. Farther north, in the Central Highlands, another theater of heavy fighting, the pattern was similar. Major U.S. operations inflicted severe casualties and kept the communists off balance. But American forces never destroyed their ability to carry on the war.

Communist advantages were even more evident in the countless small skirmishes that made up the vast majority of the fighting in South Vietnam. More than 96 percent of all firefights involved U.S. units numbering fewer than two hundred troops. In these engagements, the North Vietnamese and Vietcong—dubbed "VC" or "Victor Charlie" by U.S. GIs—almost always held the tactical advantage, choosing when and where to initiate

U.S. helicopters ferry American and South Vietnamese soldiers into action during a search-and-destroy mission southwest of Saigon in August 1967. (AP Images/Dang Van Phuoc)

combat and pulling back when losses threatened to mount too high. "You go out on patrol maybe twenty times or more, and nothin', just nothin'," one U.S. soldier complained in 1965. "Then, the twenty-first time, zap, zap, zap, you get hit and Victor Charlie fades into the jungle before you can close with him."[23] Sometimes communist forces inflicted casualties without even making contact. Between 1965 and 1970, land mines and booby traps caused 11 percent of U.S. fatalities.

These conditions took a heavy physical and psychological toll on American troops, who inhabited a world of disorienting paradoxes. On the one hand, they enjoyed remarkable comforts in their base camps, including abundant food and beer, hot showers, and rock 'n' roll music courtesy of Armed Forces Radio, all maintained by a huge staff of supply officers, cooks, mechanics, and other "rear-echelon" specialists. In all, support personnel accounted for 80 percent of all U.S. troops in Vietnam. American soldiers could also count on quick evacuation and sophisticated medical care at base hospitals if they were wounded. On the other hand, combat "grunts" endured arduous patrolling—"humping the boonies," in GI jargon—amid forbidding terrain, soaring temperatures, and torrential rain. Westmoreland's strategy compounded those problems by forcing U.S. GIs to fight a war without front lines. Morale declined as soldiers, averaging just nineteen years old, fought repeatedly over the same ground and anticipated ambushes from every direction. For many Americans, the goal became simply to survive the standard thirteen-month tour of duty and return to "the world" in one piece.

Frustrated and frightened, U.S. soldiers tended to view all Vietnamese with distrust. Instead of bolstering partnerships with anticommunist Vietnamese and winning over the uncommitted, Americans frequently alienated the local population through demeaning or aggressive behavior. This problem resulted partly from the difficulty of distinguishing Vietnamese who supported the Saigon government from those who backed the NLF. Americans rightly believed that many Vietnamese—"gooks" or "dinks" in American slang—lacked clear-cut loyalties and cooperated with the NLF when they could do so safely. Distrust lowered inhibitions against destroying property and abusing civilians. "Children were suspect, women were suspect," one American GI remembered. "It's very easy to slip into a primitive state of mind, particularly if your life is in danger and you can't trust anyone."[24]

Alienation of the Vietnamese population also resulted from the devastating economic transformation wrought by the overpowering U.S. presence. Bombing and shelling destroyed entire villages and damaged South Vietnamese agriculture, forcing American authorities to import rice into a country that had once been one of the world's leading producers. Four million peasants, about one quarter of South Vietnam's population, fled to squalid refugee camps or overcrowded urban areas. In Saigon and other cities, the rapid influx of American goods and money produced rampant inflation and a vast black market in everything from weapons to whiskey to air conditioners. Prostitution flourished wherever there were American GIs. As in the French colonial period, some Vietnamese got rich and lived well. But for many more the new economy brought poverty, crime, disease, and debasement.

THE POLITICS OF WAR

By withstanding American force above and below the seventeenth parallel, the communists neutralized Washington's greatest asset, its advantage in military technology. This accomplishment increased the likelihood that the war would be decided in the political arena, where the communists held a considerable edge. Heirs to the nationalist tradition dating back decades, the North

Vietnamese government and the NLF maintained a degree of legitimacy enjoyed by no other contender for power in the South. At the same time, the Saigon government failed to broaden its base of support, and the Johnson administration increasingly confronted hostility abroad and antiwar activism at home.

Attitudes among the South Vietnamese population during the war are difficult to gauge, largely because they tended to fluctuate with the ebb and flow of the fighting. Still, an overall pattern is discernable. After 1965, support for the NLF declined markedly in response to greater violence and rising demands for taxes, labor, and conscripts. Ebbing revolutionary enthusiasm did not, however, bring appreciable gains for the Saigon government. Data from My Thuy Phuong, a village near Hue, may suggest a larger trend. The proportion of villagers supporting the NLF dipped from 80 percent to about 50 percent during the peak years of American involvement, but those supporting the South Vietnamese government rose to 15 percent at most, whereas at least 35 percent were politically undecided.[25] In short, ordinary South Vietnamese shifted between indecision and supporting the NLF. At no point did the Saigon regime vie for broad loyalty.

Still, American policymakers persisted in their decade-old effort to create a viable South Vietnamese state. For a brief time during 1965 and 1966, they seemed to be getting somewhere. Chronic governmental instability came to an end as Nguyen Cao Ky's regime proved surprisingly durable. Optimistic that they had at last found leaders capable of sinking roots into the populace, American officials pressed Ky for reforms aimed at expanding his government's appeal. At a February 1966 summit meeting in Honolulu held to jump-start new efforts in this vein, Ky and Johnson jointly declared their dedication to win what Ky called "the heart of the people."[26]

As with so many similar undertakings in the past, the new initiative achieved little. The summit had barely ended when the

Ky regime faced a powerful surge of antigovernment agitation in many cities. As in 1963, Buddhists led the protests but quickly drew support from students and other groups hostile to the regime and its dependence on the United States. The upheaval ended only after Ky sent troops to Da Nang to quash a mutiny by soldiers loyal to the Buddhists—an act that that made a mockery of the government's professed commitment to political reform. Meanwhile, efforts to promote pacification and economic development in the countryside brought meager progress. Shortages of trained personnel, discord between Washington and Saigon, and corruption among South Vietnamese administrators bedeviled the program from the outset, as did effective countermeasures by the NLF. Johnson's decision in May 1967 to streamline the pacification effort under a single U.S. bureaucracy promised better results, but, because of foot-dragging by South Vietnamese officials, it took a year to implement the plan.

Only in one area did Saigon and Washington see tangible advances in their campaign to build up the legitimacy of the South Vietnamese state. Prodded by U.S. officials, the Ky government supervised the drafting of a new constitution and held nationwide elections. Yet even these achievements were tainted in ways that reflected widespread antipathy toward the regime. The government and its allies manipulated the constitution-writing process to assure that only staunch anticommunists could hold office and then rigged the elections held in September 1967 to ensure the outcome. Despite all these machinations, the government's candidate for president, Nguyen Van Thieu, won with just 35 percent of the popular vote, while Truong Dinh Dzu, a virtual unknown who backed negotiations with the NLF, finished second with 17 percent.

All of these failures deepened skepticism around the world about U.S. policy. In 1965 and 1966, the Johnson administration intensified its efforts to obtain troop commitments—or at least economic support or military equipment—from its allies. American policymakers believed such contributions were crucial to substantiate U.S. claims to be fighting on behalf of the entire "free world." A few Asian and Pacific countries, eager to preserve close ties with Washington, responded positively. South Korea sent sixty thousand troops in exchange for major U.S. economic concessions. Australia, New Zealand, Thailand, the Philippines, and Taiwan contributed much smaller contingents. America's most powerful allies, however, declined to help. Leaders of Britain, France, Canada, Italy, and other major U.S. partners, deeply skeptical of American policy and facing domestic pressure to steer clear of the war, acted mainly by launching or backing diplomatic initiatives to settle the war through negotiations—part of a constant quest for talks that yielded more than two thousand peace bids by governments and international organizations around the world from 1965 through 1967.[27]

These proposals created a similar dilemma for Washington and Hanoi. Both governments wished to score propaganda points by professing their desire for peace. But both also believed, despite stalemate on the battlefield, that they could achieve their aims by carrying on the fight. Each side, that is, continued to assume it would eventually find the other's breaking point. Accordingly, the U.S. and North Vietnamese governments frequently declared their openness to peace talks but hastened to spell out terms that essentially demanded surrender by the other side on the central issue, the status of South Vietnam. Hanoi insisted that the NLF control the political future of the South, whereas the United States refused to consider that possibility. Only once—a secret initiative launched by Polish and Italian officials in late 1966—did the two sides seriously consider a compromise formula. But persistent distrust between Washington and Hanoi torpedoed any possibility of a deal.

Around the world, America's reputation suffered as the war dragged on. From Sweden to India to Japan, large chunks of public opinion lauded North Vietnam as a heroic nation fighting for its independence and decried U.S. behavior, especially the bombing of the North. Far more worrying for the Johnson administration, however, was plummeting support for the war in the United States. In the early months of escalation, Johnson enjoyed relatively strong approval. Although highly motivated doves and hawks criticized his handling of the war in 1965 and 1966, big majorities of Congress and the public backed him, just as they had supported presidential decisions on national security since the Second World War. In 1967, however, antiwar activism accelerated dramatically, marking a watershed moment not only in the Vietnam War but also in the Cold War more generally. For the first time, a large percentage of the public questioned the way political leaders managed foreign affairs. By the end of the year, polls showed that 45 percent of Americans believed intervention had been a mistake.[28]

Some of Johnson's critics were hawks who believed the United States should escalate further. But many were part of the increasingly vocal antiwar movement, a diverse, fractious conglomeration of Americans who wanted to end the fighting immediately or, much more commonly, through a negotiated settlement. At one end of the spectrum were college students, pacifists, and hippies who viewed the war as a symptom of an antidemocratic mind-set that also underlay racism, sexism, materialism, and excessive obedience to authority. For these Americans, antiwar activism was often part of a larger agenda for profound social change that mobilized many young Americans during the 1960s. The United States could establish a more decent society, they believed, only by jettisoning traditional attitudes and thoroughly reforming the country. A far larger body of liberals offered a more limited critique of the war. In this view, the U.S. commitment in Vietnam represented major errors of judgment but did not flow from deeper flaws in American motives or institutions. The fighting

Antiwar protesters collect draft cards during a demonstration at the Federal Building in San Francisco, California, on October 16, 1967. (AP Images)

must stop, liberals contended, to avoid squandering America's good name and resources in a brutal conflict that could not be won at a reasonable cost.

Antiwar activism took many forms. More than half a million young men—most famously heavyweight boxing champion Muhammad Ali—defied the draft. Some burned their draft cards in solemn ceremonies organized by protest groups. Approximately fifty thousand escaped prosecution by fleeing to Canada, while others risked trial in the United States. Meanwhile, Reverend Martin Luther King Jr. and other African-American leaders lashed out in 1967 against a conflict that distracted the nation from the unfinished civil rights agenda and sent black soldiers to fight in Vietnam for liberties denied them at home. Most spectacularly, demonstrations on campuses and in cities around the country grew ever larger and more bitter, culminating in a giant protest in Washington, D.C., in fall 1967. More than seventy-five thousand activists gathered at the Lincoln Memorial on October 21 for speeches denouncing the war. "Support Our GIs, Bring Them Home Now," banners proclaimed.[29] The next day, thirty-five thousand protesters marched to the Pentagon, where radical leader Abbie Hoffman led an effort to levitate the building with mystical chants. Less whimsically, protesters pelted soldiers guarding the site with debris. Later the soldiers cracked down violently, arresting 667 protesters—the largest arrest total from any demonstration to date. The whole episode was, however, only a hint of the confrontations and controversies to come in 1968.

THE TET OFFENSIVE

"NORTHERNERS, SOUTHERNERS FACING THE Americans, advance! Victory is ours!" So declared Ho Chi Minh in a short poem he published in early 1968 to mark Tet, the Vietnamese lunar new year.[1] Communist leaders chose the holiday to launch a massive offensive throughout South Vietnam aimed at inspiring a general uprising to overthrow the Saigon government and bring the NLF to power. Just after the start of festivities, roughly eighty-four thousand troops launched surprise attacks against hundreds of cities and villages from the seventeenth parallel to the Mekong Delta. Most remarkably, a squad of NLF commandos briefly penetrated the U.S. embassy compound in Saigon, the symbolic epicenter of American power in the country.

Yet within days, U.S. and South Vietnamese forces had beaten back the onslaught almost everywhere. Some Americans contended, in fact, that the attacks had resulted in a major U.S. victory—a claim repeated by many commentators since 1968. A more accurate appraisal came from CBS newsman Walter Cronkite, who glumly asserted a month after the offensive began that the United States was "mired in stalemate."[2] Neither the communist attack nor the U.S.–South Vietnamese counterattack did anything to break the deadlock that had taken hold over the previous three years.

The offensive merely changed the nature of the stalemate. By confirming opposition to the war among the American public, it persuaded President Johnson to end his policy of gradual escalation. It also led both Washington and Hanoi, at last, to open negotiations on a settlement. But neither side abandoned its key aims in South Vietnam, and the bloodiest fighting of the war ensued during the remainder of 1968 as each continued to search for the other's breaking point.

PRELUDE

By mid-1967, the military deadlock stirred roughly analogous debates in Washington and Hanoi. In each capital, some officials, confident that the war was turning their way, favored further escalation. Others saw no chance of winning a full-fledged military victory and urged negotiations. If the terms of debate were similar, however, the decisions that resulted diverged sharply. As so often before, Johnson settled on a middle-ground solution that called essentially for more of the same. Hanoi leaders, meanwhile, opted for a huge offensive that they hoped would bring victory.

In Washington, the military led the drive to expand the U.S. war effort. Increasingly bitter about what they regarded as excessive caution among civilian leaders, Westmoreland and the Joint Chiefs of Staff pressed Johnson not only to send more troops and to intensify the bombing but also to take steps that he had so far refused—mobilization of reserve units and extension of the ground war into Cambodia, Laos, and even the southernmost parts of North Vietnam to destroy communist bases and cut the Ho Chi Minh Trail. Behind these proposals lay optimism that U.S. and South Vietnamese forces were steadily grinding down the enemy. Robert Komer, head of the reorganized pacification program, claimed particularly encouraging results, reporting in September 1967 that 68 percent of the South Vietnamese population lived under "reasonably secure conditions" and that only 17 percent of inhabited areas were controlled by the NLF. "The war is by no means over but neither is it stalemated," the U.S. command in Saigon reported to Washington. "We are steadily winning it, and the pace accelerates as we reinforce our successes and intensify our pressures."[3]

Many senior civilian officials vigorously disputed such claims. In fact, these policymakers contended, the United States was failing to achieve any of its goals. Intelligence reports showed that aerial bombing had little effect on Hanoi's will or ability to wage war. Meanwhile, CIA analysts cast doubt on claims of progress in the ground war, notably by questioning the statistics underpinning the military's optimism. Though Westmoreland claimed there were only two hundred eighty-five thousand NLF and North Vietnamese soldiers in the South, the CIA, more sensitive to the presence of irregular guerrilla forces, counted between five hundred thousand and six hundred thousand—numbers that made a mockery of military claims that U.S. forces had reached the crossover point.[4]

Skeptics also pointed to failures in the political realm. After visiting Saigon, Vice President Hubert Humphrey warned privately that the United States was "throwing lives and money down a corrupt rat hole" by backing the unpopular Thieu regime.[5] Worse yet, in the view of an increasingly disillusioned Defense Secretary McNamara, the war was damaging U.S. leadership globally. "The picture of the world's greatest superpower killing or seriously injuring 1,000 non-combatants a week, while trying to pound a tiny, backward nation into submission on an issue whose merits are hotly disputed, is not a pretty one," McNamara wrote.[6]

Once a key proponent of escalation, McNamara spoke for many officials when he called for a halt to bombing in the North. He also recommended capping the number of American ground forces, shifting to a new military strategy, and transferring the major combat burden to the South Vietnamese army, the ARVN. More fundamentally, he urged that the United States revise its war aims and seek negotiations on a compromise settlement. McNamara put the best face on his suggestions by pointing out that the Western position in Asia had improved since 1965. A right-wing coup in Indonesia had ended the communist threat in that pivotal nation, while huge turmoil within China—the consequence of Mao Zedong's catastrophic attempt to remake his country through a "Cultural Revolution"—severely weakened Beijing's ability to exert influence beyond its borders.

Confronted with bitter division among his advisers, Johnson, increasingly angry and dejected, refused both extremes and clung to the middle. He feared that bold escalation would not only fail to bring decisive results but also stir additional antiwar agitation in the United States and antagonize the communist powers. At the same time, he worried that steps toward negotiation would unleash criticism from conservatives and damage American credibility worldwide. Johnson's personal proclivities may also have fed his refusal to back down. Deeply invested in his image as a tough-minded leader, he feared for his own reputation as well as that of his party. Only in small ways was Johnson willing to alter course. In late 1967, he modified U.S. peace terms by dropping his insistence that Hanoi stop all military activity in the South before he would suspend the bombing and open negotiations. This step did not, however, reflect any change in the basic American goal: a durable, noncommunist South Vietnam.

In late 1967, in fact, Johnson showed far more eagerness to shore up domestic support for the war than to rethink his aims.

Exasperated by the antiwar movement, he ordered the CIA to start an illegal surveillance program against protest leaders. Over the next seven years, the initiative that became known as Operation Chaos collected information on three hundred thousand Americans. The Federal Bureau of Investigation, meanwhile, made efforts to infiltrate and harass the movement. The White House also sought to mobilize pro-administration opinion by establishing organizations to disseminate favorable reports about the war. More visibly, the administration brought Westmoreland back from Saigon in November 1967 to reassure the public that the war was going well—a mission he embraced warmly. "We have reached an important point where the end begins to come into view," Westmoreland declared in a much-publicized speech. Withdrawals of American troops, he suggested, might begin within two years.[7]

Johnson's decisions to stay the course coincided with decisions in Hanoi to try for sudden, decisive gains through a major offensive. As in Washington, communist policymaking during 1967 took place within a highly contentious atmosphere. Mounting death and destruction encouraged some leaders, roughly the same group that had earlier prioritized the construction of socialism in the North over military struggle in the South, to insist that Hanoi should shift to a less costly military strategy and seek negotiations. American bombing was demolishing the North Vietnamese economy, these moderates complained, while the ground war was exacting an intolerable toll in human lives.

This peace-minded faction was also emboldened by shifts within the communist bloc. Although Hanoi generally managed to maintain cooperative relations with both Moscow and Beijing despite the deepening Sino-Soviet rift, individual North Vietnamese leaders leaned toward one superpower or the other. Leaders who favored aggressive pursuit of the war usually sided with China, which, after a few peace-minded years in the 1950s, had consistently espoused revolutionary activism. Those who favored a negotiated solution generally sided with the Soviet Union, which had long advocated a peaceful road to reunification. As the Vietnam conflict escalated, the militant, pro-Chinese group controlled policymaking, while Chinese aid to North Vietnam exceeded that from the Soviet Union. By 1967, however, the balance had shifted. With China consumed by the Cultural Revolution, the Soviet Union became North Vietnam's most important patron. Pro-Moscow moderates gained new stature.

Pressure for compromise confronted the pro-Chinese militants with a serious problem: How could they rededicate their nation to the far-reaching war aims that had guided DRV policy since 1963? Their answer was the Tet Offensive and a related purge of moderates from the government. By mounting unprecedented attacks, Communist party First Secretary Le Duan and other hardliners hoped to score a decisive victory that would bring their goals within reach. Through a purge, they hoped to eliminate key opponents and to show Moscow that accepting Soviet aid did not mean accepting its conciliatory agenda. Hardliners put the scheme into operation in July 1967, when the secret police imprisoned a small group of intellectuals and journalists on trumped-up charges of conspiring against the party. Arrests of party members and government officials followed. Meanwhile, planning for what the communists called the "General Offensive and General Uprising" went forward.[8]

Superficially, leaders in Hanoi exuded optimism that the long-awaited moment—the urban uprising that had always been the end-point of communist strategy—had arrived. "Our victory is close at hand," proclaimed party instructions to local officials in the South.[9] Quietly, however, communist leaders knew they were gambling. They might achieve only a partial victory without ending the war, or, in the worst case, they might provoke the

United States to expand the conflict. Anxious about heavy losses, Hanoi assigned the bulk of the fighting to NLF units rather than to the North Vietnamese army. Still, communist military strength in the South, along with the unpopularity of the Saigon regime and the fragility of American public opinion, gave Hanoi reason to believe it could land what party leaders called "thundering blows" that would "change the face of the war."[10]

ATTACK AND COUNTERATTACK

Military preparations for the offensive began in October 1967, when communist troops launched attacks in remote areas. Their objective was to lure U.S. forces away from densely populated regions that were the ultimate target. American and ARVN troops prevailed in heavy fighting at Dak To in the Central Highlands, Song Be and Loc Ninh near Cambodia, and elsewhere. But the communists achieved their goal of inducing Westmoreland to thin his forces near Saigon and along the coast. Assuming that communist ambitions were focused on the northernmost provinces, Westmoreland sent especially heavy reinforcements to Khe Sanh, an isolated U.S. Marine base besieged by North Vietnamese troops. Commanders of U.S. forces, along with the American media and President Johnson, fixated for several weeks on the savage fighting there, convinced that Hanoi aimed to score a victory akin to the triumph at Dien Bien Phu in 1954.

With American attention thus distracted, communists prepared for the urban attacks scheduled to coincide with Tet, a holiday for which both sides had observed a cease-fire in previous years. NLF troops, sometimes disguised as ordinary peasants or even as South Vietnamese soldiers, moved into the cities and stockpiled weapons, while political operatives plotted assassinations of South Vietnamese officials and readied themselves to lead a popular uprising.

The Tet attacks commenced in the wee hours of January 30, inaugurating the Year of the Monkey with a monumental burst of fighting. Within hours, communist forces had struck five of six major cities, thirty-six of forty-four provincial capitals, and sixty-four district capitals. In Saigon, nineteen NLF soldiers blew a hole in the wall surrounding the U.S. embassy at 2:45 a.m. and waged a six-hour firefight with Marine guards before being killed or wounded. Other NLF units attacked the Saigon airport, President Thieu's palace, and the national radio station. Far to the north, about seventy-five hundred communist troops seized the old imperial capital of Hue.

Reports from U.S. intelligence services had indicated for some weeks that an attack might be coming, and Westmoreland had persuaded South Vietnamese leaders to keep half their forces on duty during the holiday. On the whole, though, U.S. commanders, exaggerating the degree to which they had weakened the enemy, had little inkling of what lay in store. The Tet Offensive was, lamented one National Security Council aide, "the worst intelligence failure of the war."[11] In many places, the element of surprise enabled the communists to land quick blows that sent the ARVN reeling.

Sudden communist gains did not, however, add up to a decisive breakthrough. To the contrary, U.S. and ARVN forces recovered quickly and reversed enemy advances almost everywhere within days. Only in Hue did the attackers manage to hold their ground considerably longer. American Marines and ARVN units finally recaptured the city on March 2 after four weeks of horrific house-to-house combat that killed five hundred U.S. and South Vietnamese soldiers, along with perhaps ten times as many communist troops. Overall, the offensive brought massively disproportionate losses on the communist side. From January 29 to

March 31, the NLF and the North Vietnamese army suffered as many as fifty-eight thousand dead, while about thirty-four hundred U.S. and ARVN soldiers were killed or wounded. Washington took heart from such numbers and from the surprisingly strong performance by the ARVN, which, far from cracking under pressure, fought with determination in many places.

There was more bad news for the communists: the offensive failed to produce any popular uprising. Though the NLF extended its control in rural areas and crippled pacification efforts, the party's grand hopes for the cities came to naught. Part of the problem was that the U.S.–South Vietnamese counterattack pushed communist forces back before cadres had a chance to begin mobilizing the population and tear down Saigon's administrative apparatus. Only in Hue did they have time to set up a new government and to eliminate political opponents, a campaign that led to the brutal execution of some twenty-eight hundred South Vietnamese soldiers and civilians. The larger problem, though, appears to have been a general lack of enthusiasm for the communist cause. The cities had been the revolutionaries' weak spot for half a century, and little had changed by 1968.

In one way, moreover, the Tet Offensive appreciably worsened the communists' prospects. During the hopeful first hours of the attacks, many NLF operatives came out into the open for the first time. When U.S. and South Vietnamese forces retook the cities, they had little difficulty capturing or killing those individuals. Meanwhile, NLF units bore the brunt of the U.S.–South Vietnamese counterattack. The overall effect was to decimate the NLF and to enable Northerners to dominate the revolutionary movement in the South more fully than ever before. That change undoubtedly strengthened Hanoi's ability to control the war, but it also contributed to declining revolutionary enthusiasm in the South by confirming suspicions that the North aimed simply to take over South Vietnam.

U.S. Marines huddle behind a tree on February 4, 1968, during intense fighting to dislodge communist forces from Hue. (AP Images)

In one crucial respect, however, the Tet Offensive was an unqualified success for the communists. As they had hoped, the onslaught produced powerful shock waves in the United States, where many policymakers and much of the American public saw it as stark evidence that the war could not be won at a reasonable cost. Westmoreland and Johnson described the offensive as a desperate move by a badly weakened enemy and proclaimed it a U.S. victory. But many Americans would have none of it. More characteristic of the national mood was the response of news anchor Walter Cronkite. "What the hell is going on?" he exclaimed. "I thought we were winning the war!"[12] The sheer scale and intensity of the attacks flew in the face of repeated reassurances by Westmoreland and other officials that the communists were nearly defeated. A stream of media reports and images describing spectacular carnage suggested that the United States was embroiled in a brutal, dehumanizing struggle. For example, newspapers and television programs across the country carried gruesome images of the South Vietnamese national police chief executing an NLF prisoner with a shot to the head.

Media reports exaggerated communist gains in the first days of the offensive, but they did not, as many critics would later contend, lead Americans to turn dramatically against the war in a way that prevented policymakers from capitalizing on the successful counterattack. In fact, the Tet Offensive produced no dramatic plunge in public support for the war. Polls showed only a continuation of the gradual decline of support that had begun a year earlier. Moreover, many American officials, including some military commanders, shared the media's bleak view of the war. "We suffered a loss, there can be no doubt about it," admitted Army Chief of Staff Harold K. Johnson.[13] American leaders knew that the offensive had crippled American pacification programs. They also worried that the South Vietnamese government had

In an image that shocked many Americans, South Vietnamese national police chief Nguyen Ngoc Loan executes an NLF prisoner in Saigon on February 1, 1968. (AP Images/Eddie Adams)

suffered a grievous blow and wondered whether the ARVN could stand up to more hard fighting.

NEW DELIBERATIONS

Soaring anxiety within the Johnson administration sparked a new round of deliberations that rehashed, albeit at a much higher level of urgency, the 1967 debate between proponents of escalation and de-escalation. As before, the military argued for a vast expansion of the war. Westmoreland and the Joint Chiefs of Staff asked President Johnson to send two hundred six thousand more troops and renewed their appeals to mobilize American reserve forces and to permit ground attacks into Cambodia, Laos, and the southernmost strip of North Vietnam. Such an escalation would, the generals insisted, enable U.S. forces to build on the successful Tet counterattacks and cripple the communists. Without it, they contended, the U.S. war effort faced uncertain prospects.

Johnson sent ten thousand five hundred additional troops to Vietnam immediately after the offensive began, but, as in 1967, he balked at the military's sweeping proposals. Uncertain how to proceed, he ordered his new secretary of defense, Clark Clifford, to undertake an "A to Z" reassessment of U.S. policy.[14] Clifford, appointed to replace McNamara, quickly arrived at many of the same conclusions that had disillusioned his predecessor. He advised the president to reject the huge troop request. Such an escalation, Clifford warned, would increase bloodshed and domestic strife with no assurance of military progress. In fact, Clifford counseled, there was little reason to believe that the United States could achieve victory with "double or triple" the troops the military had requested. "We put in more—they match it. We put in more—they match," he warned Johnson. Additionally, Clifford voiced worries that an expanded war would seriously damage the American economy and undermine the country's ability to sustain its military commitments elsewhere in the world. He advised the president to send a mere twenty-two thousand more troops to fill immediate needs but otherwise to press the South Vietnamese to assume a greater share of the fighting.[15]

In most ways, the president leaned toward Clifford's view as he mulled over his options in February and March. He readily accepted Clifford's advice to reject the military's troop request and to transfer greater combat responsibility to South Vietnam. Johnson even went beyond these proposals by toying with a suggestion from Secretary of State Rusk to cut back sharply on bombing of the North to test Hanoi's interest in negotiation and ease antiwar agitation. Yet the president sided with the military in one subtle but crucial respect. He believed that the Tet counterattacks had badly weakened the communists and that U.S. and ARVN forces held the upper hand. Johnson reasoned, therefore, that capping escalation and opening negotiations did not mean abandoning long-standing war aims. He might be able to achieve his goals while reining in the American commitment.

Johnson maintained that belief even as three developments during March underscored the urgency of de-escalation and threatened his campaign for reelection in November. First, antiwar activism, far from declining as time passed, accelerated, especially after the *New York Times* revealed the military's request for two hundred six thousand troops, kept secret until then. Although Johnson had already rejected that proposal, it touched off a massive outcry in Congress, where both hawks and doves blasted the administration. The president's troubles deepened on March 12, when Senator Eugene McCarthy of Minnesota, challenging Johnson for the Democratic nomination on an antiwar platform, won 42 percent of the vote in the New Hampshire primary. Most of McCarthy's votes came from disgruntled hawks, but the outcome was taken as a sign that Johnson was losing the support of his party. Four days later, the challenge to Johnson intensified dramatically when a longtime rival, New York senator Robert F. Kennedy, entered the race calling for peace in Vietnam.

Second, evidence mounted that the war was severely damaging the American economy. In 1965, administration officials believed that the country could pay for both a limited war in Vietnam and Great Society social programs. By 1968, however, economists had changed their minds. The cost of the war—more than $2 billion per month in 1967—ran far higher than anticipated, causing mounting deficits and inflation. Declining confidence in U.S. currency led foreign investors to exchange dollars for gold, culminating in a sell-off of $372 million of gold on March 14, 1968, and the closing of the international gold market—a stunning event that signaled the drastic weakening of the U.S. economy. Treasury Secretary Henry Fowler warned Johnson that major escalation in Vietnam would require a big tax increase and deep cuts in Great Society programs in order to avoid an international financial debacle.

Third, a panel of independent foreign policy experts called together by the president, the so-called Wise Men, arrived at a gloomy assessment of the war and its effects on the nation's international standing. At a meeting before the Tet Offensive, the committee had generally backed the administration's handling of the war. Upon reviewing the post-Tet situation, however, it offered a starkly different conclusion. The group not only recommended against further troop commitments but also urged the president to stop bombing the North and to consider how to negotiate a withdrawal from South Vietnam. Far more than protests on campuses or in the streets, the defection of these powerful men—all of them from the business, legal, and policy-making elite—convinced Johnson that he had to do something dramatic.

These setbacks helped set the stage for a landmark speech about the war that Johnson delivered before a nationwide television audience on March 31. He announced a new troop deployment of thirteen thousand five hundred soldiers and, displaying sensitivity to the nation's economic crisis, asked Congress to pass a tax increase to pay for it. But mostly Johnson described plans to de-escalate the war. "We are prepared to move immediately toward peace through negotiations," he declared. As a "first step," he continued, he was ordering an end to all bombing of North Vietnam except in the area just above the seventeenth parallel, where communist activities were most threatening to American troops. He also announced that he was appointing veteran diplomat Averell Harriman as chief U.S. negotiator in any talks that could be arranged. In his breathtaking conclusion, Johnson declared that he would neither seek nor accept the Democratic nomination for president later that year. He would devote all of his time, he promised, to the war and other problems confronting the nation.[16]

STALEMATE RENEWED

Johnson's speech seemed to herald peace. Three days later, Hanoi agreed to open talks, and governments around the world expressed hope for a deal. In fact, however, commitments to start talks did not mean that either side was willing to back down from key war aims. Indeed, in a less noted part of his speech, Johnson made clear that U.S. forces would be pulled out of Vietnam only in return for a North Vietnamese withdrawal from the South and an end to infiltration—demands that the United States had maintained for years. When Hanoi surprised him by agreeing to talks, Johnson continued to hope that U.S.–ARVN gains on the battlefield would force the communists to make all the concessions at the bargaining table. The commitment to negotiate was, therefore, more a tactical adjustment in pursuit of old objectives than a bold step toward disengagement.

In Hanoi, communist leaders thought in similar terms. Disappointed with the results of the Tet Offensive, they were willing to accept negotiations as the best way to secure quick American concessions, especially a full stop to bombing above the seventeenth parallel.[17] But the Hanoi regime, still dominated by the militants who had adamantly rejected talks in 1967, viewed negotiations mainly as a forum for consolidating gains yet to be secured on the battlefield and through deteriorating support for the war within the United States. "We will discuss peace in our own way, . . . in the position of a winner, not as a loser," asserted one North Vietnamese government memorandum.[18] Hanoi aimed to achieve its maximum war aims by inflicting losses that would exacerbate controversy in American society and ultimately force Washington to capitulate.

With neither side interested in compromise, the talks went nowhere. Before discussions even started, in fact, Washington and Hanoi clashed over where the meetings should take place. They finally settled on Paris, where negotiations opened on May 13 amid intense international media coverage. But deadlock quickly set in on the issue that would remain the key sticking point for months. North Vietnamese negotiators demanded that Washington stop all bombing above the seventeenth parallel before they would agree to talk about anything else. The U.S. delegation insisted that bombing would cease only in return for North Vietnamese agreement to stop infiltration and to withdraw troops from the South.

Clifford and Harriman begged Johnson to offer concessions to get the talks moving and begin the process of winding down the war. But the president, buoyed by the military, Rusk, and National Security Adviser Walt Rostow, refused to give any ground. Indeed, deeply embittered by the impending end of his presidency and humiliated by the prospect of defeat in Vietnam, Johnson increasingly scorned doves within his own party who had, he complained, led him into war only to abandon him when the going got tough. Factionalism permeated Washington as the Democratic Party split ever more rancorously over the war. Desperate to show that he had been right all along, the president spoke privately of his desire to pummel North Vietnam as never before and insisted that military gains since the Tet Offensive would yield major advances at the negotiating table as long as he was patient enough to wait for them.

Hoping to capitalize on their post-Tet momentum, U.S. forces intensified operations throughout 1968, making it the bloodiest year of the war. More than fourteen thousand five hundred U.S.

soldiers were killed and forty-six thousand wounded, while the communists lost an estimated sixty thousand killed and one hundred twenty thousand wounded. While much of the fighting followed familiar patterns, Johnson and the military increasingly pinned their hopes on two major changes in the conduct of the ground war. First, the military adopted a new strategy designed to neutralize communist political advantages and to strengthen the U.S. hand in Paris by extending control over as much of South Vietnam as possible. The shift began in March, when the Johnson administration removed Westmoreland as U.S. commander in Vietnam. His replacement, General Creighton Abrams, called for a new approach that centered on providing security for the South Vietnamese population—precisely what Westmoreland's critics had long urged. The strategy changed the main role of U.S. ground troops from killing enemy soldiers to driving them out of populated areas and then establishing lines behind which pacification programs might succeed in extirpating communist influence. For the first time, the U.S. command assigned a high priority to destroying the insurgency's political apparatus. Under the Chieu Hoi (Open Arms) program, South Vietnam offered amnesty to NLF defectors. Under the Phoenix Program, meanwhile, U.S. and South Vietnamese intelligence operatives targeted communists for arrest or assassination.

Second, Washington began shifting more of the combat burden onto the ARVN, the first steps of what Americans would later call the "Vietnamization" of the fighting. The program stemmed partly from a desire to blunt domestic opposition to the war by cutting U.S. casualties. But it sprang as well from determination to put more troops in the field and to create a force that could maintain security once American soldiers went home. The program appealed, in short, to both factions of American policymakers—those who wanted to wind down the war and those who insisted on escalating it. Washington provided aid to expand the ARVN from six hundred eighty-five thousand soldiers to more than eight hundred thousand and to equip them with the most modern weapons.

Major U.S. operations, intensified pacification, and the beefed-up ARVN brought notable results. American and South Vietnamese forces extended control into new areas. The Phoenix Program, which ultimately eliminated an estimated thirty-four thousand insurgents, damaged the communist political network in many areas. Morale among communist forces suffered as casualties piled up and as victory seemed more distant than ever. Relations between insurgents and the Southern peasantry deteriorated to new lows as the communists resorted to ever more coercive methods to find recruits and collect taxes. In the North, too, the population soured on the war as it devoured a generation of young men. "It began to seem like an open pit," recalled one North Vietnamese journalist. "There was even a kind of motto that the whole generation of army-age North Vietnamese adopted— they tattooed it on themselves and they sang songs about it—'Born in the North, to die in the South.' "[19] North Vietnamese draftees, like their American counterparts, increasingly sought medical deferments, and a few mutilated their own bodies to avoid service.

Mounting problems for the communists did not mean, however, that the United States had belatedly found the formula for victory in Vietnam, as some commentators would later argue. Washington and Saigon still confronted formidable military and political problems. For one thing, ferocious American bombing failed, as in earlier days, to stop North Vietnam from sending troops and matériel into the South to offset losses. In South Vietnam's villages and hamlets, much of the communist infrastructure—the local committees, militias, and intelligence networks that sustained the insurgency at the rice-roots level— managed to survive the pacification effort despite suffering serious damage.

Meanwhile, a shifting array of weaknesses continued to bedevil the government in Saigon. By a few measures, the Thieu regime improved its performance during 1968. It initiated efforts to fight corruption and inflation and mobilized city-dwellers to repair damage caused by the Tet attacks. In other ways, however, the government suffered setbacks. The Tet fighting created a million new refugees, compounding the country's staggering social crisis. The ARVN, following its impressive performance in beating back the offensive, slipped back into old patterns of corruption and passivity. Desertion rates reached all-time highs. For his part, Thieu, perpetually suspicious of his rivals and unwilling to broaden the base of his government, did little to expand his government's appeal.

For all these reasons, the United States failed to achieve the breakthrough that Johnson desperately desired. The overall result of the Tet fighting was to weaken both sides and to establish a new kind of stalemate—one at the negotiating table as well as on the battlefield—by the middle of 1968. Dramatic change came only on the American home front, where antiwar activism reached new levels of intensity after Tet. On college campuses, demonstrations grew more numerous and violent in the spring as many student groups embraced more radical positions. Brutal clashes between protesters and police, along with the assassination of Martin Luther King Jr. and the race riots that ensued in many cities, convinced many Americans that the foundation of their society was cracking. Robert F. Kennedy's assassination on June 6 sent the country reeling anew, but the sense of national crisis peaked with the Democratic Party's national convention in August. Leading up to the convention, antiwar leaders spoke of their hopes to assemble as many as two hundred thousand demonstrators and threatened an array of attention-grabbing activities, ranging from mass burning of draft cards to mass sex in city parks. In the event, only about ten thousand protesters took part, but the results were even more stunning than promised. While party delegates clashed over the war inside the convention hall, protesters and police waged harrowing street battles that received wide media coverage. In all, the rioting resulted in 668 arrests, one death, and hundreds of injuries.[20]

The violence dismayed Johnson, but it did not lead him to shift course in Vietnam. On the contrary, he worked hard to ensure that the convention endorsed his conduct of the war. Through his last day in office, in fact, Johnson refused to give up on accomplishing his aims in Vietnam. As in the past, he agreed only to tactical adjustments designed to relieve political pressure. By far the most important such shift came as the campaign to succeed him heated up in October. Polls showed the Democratic nominee, Vice President Humphrey, badly trailing the Republican candidate, former Vice President Richard M. Nixon. To rescue Humphrey and other Democrats running for office, party leaders urged the president to make a dramatic peace gesture. Johnson still resented the peace faction within his party and showed special wrath for Humphrey, who had broken ranks by calling publicly for a bombing halt. But Johnson finally gave in, agreeing in October that U.S. negotiators could offer an end to all bombing of North Vietnam. He did so, though, only after satisfying himself that a bombing halt would not imperil the battlefield situation and assuring commanders that they could compensate by intensifying attacks on the Ho Chi Minh Trail in southern Laos. He also demanded that Hanoi agree to limit infiltration and allow the Saigon government to take part in the Paris talks.

North Vietnamese officials grudgingly accepted Johnson's terms, though they studiously avoided any specific commitments. This change reflected Hanoi's definitive judgment that the Tet Offensive, consisting of the January onslaught as well as follow-up attacks through the spring and summer, had not yielded as strong a negotiating position as the communists had hoped. The shift also reflected Hanoi's calculations about American politics. North Vietnamese leaders believed that the Democrats, desperate to show progress toward ending the war in order to boost Humphrey's campaign, would prove much more agreeable negotiating partners than a new Republican administration led by Nixon, well known as a fierce anticommunist. Motivated in these ways, Hanoi leaders embraced a new approach to the war that they dubbed "talking while fighting."[21]

Only one obstacle prevented Johnson from announcing the deal and Humphrey from trying to reap the political reward. The Saigon government, fearing that Washington would sacrifice South Vietnamese interests in its politically inspired bid for peace, rejected the terms offered by Johnson. Nguyen Van Thieu's attitude presumably pleased Nixon. In a flagrantly unethical act, the Republican campaign had used secret intermediaries to encourage Thieu to torpedo the deal by assuring him that Nixon would defend his interests better than Humphrey would. Thieu's attitude infuriated Johnson, who confronted a painful dilemma. Should he respect Saigon's position and thus lose an opportunity to help his party score points with an electorate eager to end the war? Or should he ignore Saigon and announce the arrangement with Hanoi? Johnson attempted to split the difference. Without securing Saigon's consent, he proclaimed a total bombing halt over North Vietnam in a speech to the nation on October 31. Secretly, he also sought to reassure Thieu that the United States would take South Vietnamese interests to heart. The ploy failed. On November 1, three days before the U.S. election, Thieu announced that his government would not take part in the Paris talks. As the prospect of peace evaporated, Humphrey's chances of a comeback victory faded. Nixon won the presidency by 510,000 votes out of 73 million cast. The Republicans would take charge of the war.

Ending the
American War

During the 1968 presidential campaign, Republican nominee Richard Nixon promised to end the war in Vietnam. But he also pledged to achieve "peace with honor"—a settlement, in other words, that would secure the basic aims for which the United States had been fighting all along. The key to salvaging American goals, Nixon declared, would be to pursue new diplomatic and military approaches to the war. "One of the advantages of a new president," he declared, "is that he can start fresh without being imprisoned by the formulas of the past."[1]

Over the following years, Nixon tried a variety of novel expedients to achieve peace on American terms, variously employing escalation and withdrawal, bold gestures and secret maneuvers. At every turn, however, the new administration ran up against old problems. Though badly damaged, communist forces refused to buckle. Though apparently stable, the South Vietnamese government failed to gain support among its people. Though relieved by declining U.S. casualties, the American public and Congress continued to sour on the war.

Frustrated and bitter, Nixon finally signed a peace accord in early 1973. The administration claimed to be satisfied with the deal, which preserved an independent South Vietnam. But there could be little doubt that Nixon, desperate to pull the United States out of the Vietnam morass, had accepted a disadvantageous agreement that left the door open to a future communist victory. A pall of uncertainty hung over South Vietnam, along with neighboring Cambodia and Laos, as U.S. troops went home.

NEW APPROACHES, OLD PROBLEMS

When he assumed the presidency in January 1969, Nixon aimed to end the war in a matter of months. Like most Republicans, he had once championed American intervention, but his thinking had changed. He understood that the war was causing intolerable economic setbacks and social turmoil. At least as important, he feared that continued fighting would prevent him from achieving his highest priority, a more peaceful international order based on cooperative relations among the great powers. Nixon had watched the war destroy his predecessor and vowed to avoid that fate. "I'm not going to end up like LBJ ..., holed up in the White House, afraid to show my face on the street," Nixon declared. "I'm going to stop that war. Fast. I mean it!"[2]

But Nixon was convinced that he could not simply withdraw from the war. An outspoken anticommunist who had once assailed Democrats for "losing" China, Nixon feared partisan attack if he accepted a communist victory in Vietnam. It was not only his political prospects, however, that concerned Nixon. Even more than his Democratic predecessors, he believed that the stature of the United States around the world depended on the way he managed the war. If Washington walked away from Vietnam, Nixon thought, allies around the world would question

U.S. commitments to their security, and the communist bloc would be emboldened to challenge U.S. interests everywhere. Nothing less than the ability of the United States to function effectively in the diplomatic arena seemed to be at stake.

Nixon's outlook meshed neatly with that of his national security adviser and key partner in foreign policy, Henry Kissinger. They were an unlikely duo. Nixon, son of a California grocer, identified with middle America and seethed with resentment against East Coast intellectuals. Kissinger, a Jew born in Nazi Germany, had come to prominence as a scholar of international politics at Harvard University. On a deeper level, though, the two men saw eye to eye. Like Nixon, Kissinger craved approval and loathed his adversaries. Kissinger also shared the president's eagerness for a more harmonious international order as well as his anxiety about preserving American "credibility." No less than Nixon, Kissinger insisted the United States must "close the conflict with dignity."[3]

The only way to achieve that goal, Nixon and Kissinger believed, was to attain the central objective the United States had sought for years—an independent and secure South Vietnam. For various reasons, the two men were optimistic they could accomplish what had eluded their predecessors. Most important, they were confident that the military and political situation was better than it had been in years. The Thieu government remained stable, while U.S. and South Vietnamese forces continued to extend Saigon's control over the countryside.

The administration's hopes for further progress rested on various innovations aimed at pushing North Vietnam either to seek peace or simply to give up the fight. First, Nixon and Kissinger intended to isolate North Vietnam diplomatically by inducing Moscow to support peace on American terms. The scheme depended on Moscow's keen desire to open negotiations with Washington to curb the arms race and improve trade relations. In exchange for talks on those topics, Nixon and Kissinger would demand Soviet help in pressing North Vietnam to back down. Second, the two men aimed to intimidate the communists by using force in ways that Johnson had refused to allow. Under what he dubbed the "madman theory," Nixon hoped to convey to Hanoi that he would not hesitate to unleash America's full military might. His key asset in this endeavor was his reputation as a diehard hawk. "They'll believe any threat of force that Nixon makes because it's Nixon," the president boasted.[4]

To buy time for these strategies to take effect, Nixon sought to ease domestic unrest by gradually withdrawing American troops. U.S. officials naturally worried that pullouts would encourage North Vietnamese leaders to believe that to achieve victory they need only wait for the Americans to go home. But Nixon insisted that cuts in the number of troops could be offset by intensification of efforts begun under Johnson to build up the South Vietnamese military to fight effectively on its own. Indeed, the Nixon administration elevated the substitution of South Vietnamese soldiers for Americans to a central position in its overall approach to the war and gave it a name, "Vietnamization."

With the American public and Congress watching expectantly, Nixon and Kissinger implemented this array of stratagems in the first half of 1969. They told Moscow that opening arms talks depended on Soviet help in securing peace in Vietnam. They then upped the military ante by initiating a major bombing campaign against communist bases in eastern Cambodia. Johnson, wary of spreading the war beyond Vietnam, had rejected such a move. Nixon shared his predecessor's concern that the bombing would spark a major outcry and kept it secret. But he hoped bombing would pay off by disrupting communist military operations and signaling Hanoi that he would not be bound by earlier restraints. Meanwhile, the new administration dramatically stepped up supplies to the ARVN and, on June 8, announced plans to bring home twenty-five thousand American troops, with more to follow. Indeed, Nixon announced a general policy of providing military equipment to U.S. allies in lieu of committing American troops— an approach dubbed the "Nixon Doctrine."

None of these moves brought significant results. Militarily, American and South Vietnamese forces failed to inflict decisive blows. To be sure, setbacks in 1968 had badly weakened communist forces, leaving commanders little choice but to assume a defensive posture. "Shortcomings and weak points" had to be resolved at all levels of the communist movement, North Vietnamese leaders admitted.[5] Morale among communist forces sagged. "We want to encourage one another," a North Vietnamese doctor serving in the South wrote in her diary on June 11, 1969, "but there are moments when our worries become clear and undeniable, and the shadow of pessimism creeps upon us."[6] Meanwhile, intensified pacification programs continued to unravel the communist political apparatus in South Vietnam, and a massive exodus of refugees from rural areas made it harder than ever to find recruits and collect taxes. But setbacks did not mean defeat. In 1969, a bleak year for the communists, more than eighty thousand North Vietnamese troops marched down the Ho Chi Minh Trail to offset losses.[7]

Even in their weakened condition, North Vietnamese leaders calculated they had more to gain by continuing the fight than by making peace. They believed they needed time—possibly two or three years—to recover sufficiently to retake the offensive and negotiate from a position of strength. They also reckoned that accelerating public discontent in the United States would ultimately force Nixon to make peace on communist terms. Guided by these considerations, North Vietnamese negotiators rebuffed U.S. proposals for mutual troop withdrawals from South Vietnam. Hanoi accepted only one American idea, agreeing to establish a secret channel of communication outside the ongoing Paris talks.

North Vietnamese leaders gave no sign, however, that such contacts would produce results. Hanoi merely restated its demands: U.S. withdrawal from South Vietnam and the creation of a coalition government excluding Thieu. In a further gesture of defiance, the NLF established a Provisional Revolutionary Government to rival the Saigon regime and to administer the South following a communist victory.

Nixon's hope for a quick breakthrough also foundered on his failure to persuade Moscow to pressure Hanoi. The effort failed partly because the Soviet Union enjoyed less sway in North Vietnam than Americans assumed. Washington's hopes were dashed too by the dynamics of the ever-deepening Sino-Soviet rivalry. More eager than ever to display revolutionary ardor, Chinese diplomats urged Hanoi to shun negotiations. "We have to rely on fighting with a view to annihilating the enemy," one Chinese Politburo member advised Hanoi.[8] With their archrivals pressing for total military victory, Moscow leaders feared losing stature in the communist bloc if they pressed Hanoi to accept less. Indeed, hoping to displace China as North Vietnam's most important ally, the Soviet Union only increased its aid.

Nixon found no greater success in his bid to ease domestic turmoil. Antiwar agitation surged anew in 1969 as hopes of an early settlement faded. In Congress, Democrats attacked Nixon for failing to follow through on his promise of peace. In the streets and on campuses, meanwhile, demonstrations grew to unprecedented scale, culminating on October 15, when as many as two million Americans participated in a nationwide protest known as the Moratorium. In an unmistakable sign of widening disaffection, demonstrators increasingly eschewed the violence and youthful radicalism that had characterized much of the earlier antiwar activism. Instead, the Moratorium, like another round of nationwide protests a month later, was dominated by middle-class moderates upset by the slow pace of American withdrawal from the war.

CONTRACTION AND EXPANSION

Frustrated and angry, Nixon responded to his early failures not by modifying U.S. policy but by defiantly pressing ahead with the same mix of withdrawal, Vietnamization, diplomatic coercion, and bold military moves. Further effort in each of these areas, he hoped, would yield a favorable settlement. As in previous years, American officials believed that success was just a matter of persevering until Hanoi bent to American will.

To contain domestic turmoil, Nixon cut the number of U.S. troops in South Vietnam to 475,200 by the end of 1969 and to 334,600 a year later. He also aimed to ease domestic controversy by reforming the draft. The Selective Service System, established in 1948, had come under heavy fire for producing a military consisting disproportionately of minorities and the poor, who often lacked resources to obtain educational or medical deferments common among more affluent draftees. Nixon established a new scheme that assigned every eighteen-year-old male a draft priority through a random lottery. The switch, along with sharply declining needs for troops in the early 1970s, largely eliminated the draft as a source of discontent.

Not all of Nixon's efforts to quash dissent were so conciliatory. As antiwar activism surged in late 1969, the president railed against the "rabble in the street" and ordered the FBI and CIA to expand their harassment of antiwar organizations.[9] The administration also worked hard to exploit class cleavages, tarring critics of the war as unpatriotic elitists while insisting that less privileged Americans dutifully supported the war—a myth that would persist long after the fighting ended. Vice President Spiro Agnew blasted antiwar activists as "snobs" who "mock the common man's pride in his work, his family and his country."[10] Nixon took the higher road in a nationally televised speech, appealing for support from the "great silent majority" that, he claimed, backed the government while the unrepresentative few dominated the head-lines.[11] No such majority in fact existed among the deeply frac-tured public, but the rhetorical maneuver momentarily eased pressure on the White House.

The Vietnamization program, meanwhile, gradually trans-formed the ARVN into one of the largest and best-equipped mili-taries in the world. To be sure, the Saigon government fretted that Vietnamization was a mere rationalization for U.S. abandonment, and many American officials worried that no amount of aid could transform the ARVN into a force that would fight effectively once U.S. troops were gone. But the numbers were undeniably impres-sive. Washington provided more than a million M-16 rifles, along with enormous quantities of vehicles, planes, and helicopters. American aid also enabled South Vietnam to expand the ARVN from eight hundred fifty thousand soldiers to more than one million by 1971, while increasing salaries and benefits.[12]

The Saigon government's control over as much as 80 percent of the countryside created new opportunities for rural develop-ment projects designed to erode communist influence. South Vietnam, with U.S. funding and guidance, built new schools and hospitals. In 1970, Thieu also unveiled the "Land to the Tiller" program—the most ambitious land-redistribution scheme yet attempted in South Vietnam. The plan ultimately divvied up more than 1.5 million acres on terms comparable with those offered by the communists in earlier years.

As these programs went forward in South Vietnam, Nixon also moved boldly in the diplomatic arena. Disappointed with Mos-cow's failure to influence North Vietnam, he embraced a far more radical possibility: inducing the Chinese government to press Hanoi for peace. Sino-American relations had been frozen in fierce hostility since 1949, and few Americans had done more to stoke anti-Chinese fervor during the 1950s and 1960s than Nixon. By the time he became president, however, he had begun toying with the idea of rapprochement. Chinese leaders, eager to bolster their international legitimacy, were thinking along the same lines. For both sides, improved relations promised to help contain the Soviet Union, which had become an ever fiercer rival for China than for the United States. Indeed, Moscow and Beijing stood at the brink of war in August 1969. For Nixon, restored ties with China also carried the possibility of the same sort of deal he wanted from the Soviets. The United States would offer concessions on the status of Taiwan and other matters of concern to Beijing in return for Chinese support in ending the Vietnam War on American terms. In deepest secrecy, U.S. and Chinese representatives opened exploratory talks in late 1969.

Nixon remained convinced, however, that the best hope of coercing Hanoi lay in drastic military action. In July 1969, he informed the North Vietnamese government through French intermediaries that he would employ "measures of great consequence and force" if there was no progress toward peace by November 1. Kissinger then assembled a committee to consider how to deliver on the threat. "I can't believe that a fourth-rate power like North Vietnam doesn't have a breaking point," Kissinger declared.[13] Within weeks, the president was given a range of options codenamed Duck Hook. At the milder end, the program called for heavy bombing of North Vietnamese cities and use of anti-ship mines in Haiphong harbor, a major entry point for foreign supplies. Among more extreme options, the program suggested bombing the Red River dikes to cause devastating floods and even broached the use of tactical nuclear weapons.

Although incensed when Hanoi spurned his ultimatum, Nixon grudgingly heeded appeals from senior advisers to shelve Duck Hook. Carrying out the plan, warned Secretary of Defense Melvin Laird, would only fuel a huge public outcry; Kissinger agreed that it was unlikely to produce a breakthrough. But Nixon did not lose interest in a bold strike. In fact, his zeal only grew amid warnings from U.S. commanders that American troop withdrawals were imperiling South Vietnam's survival. Nixon's opportunity came in March 1970, when the neutralist government of Cambodia was overthrown in a coup led by a pro-American general, Lon Nol. Through years of delicate diplomacy, Cambodia's Prince Sihanouk had managed to avoid deep embroilment in the Vietnam War. The coup ended that state of affairs, starting Cambodia down a road to national catastrophe.

Nixon responded to the coup by sending aid to help Lon Nol fight both Cambodian communists known as the Khmer Rouge and the Vietnamese communists occupying the country's eastern border areas. Freed from earlier concerns about violating a neutral country, Nixon also approved one of the most controversial military operations of the war. At the end of April 1970, fifty thousand ARVN and thirty thousand U.S. troops invaded Cambodia with the aim of destroying communist bases and delivering the message that Hanoi still faced a determined foe. Many administration officials strongly opposed the operation, but Nixon, obsessed with showing toughness, insisted the moment was ripe to "go for all the marbles."[14]

In some ways, the operation was successful. Invading troops captured large quantities of equipment and food and may have set back communist military planning by a year or more. By other measures, the invasion was a disaster. Instead of destroying Vietnamese communist forces, it pushed them farther into the Cambodian interior, where they invigorated the Khmer Rouge. At the same time, the invasion sparked an unprecedented political explosion in the United States. The initial rumble of protest escalated into a nationwide crisis when members of the Ohio National Guard shot thirteen students, killing four, during a protest at Kent State University on May 4.

Over the next few weeks, more than four million college students took part in demonstrations against the war. About one-fifth of the nation's campuses closed, in some cases for the rest of the spring. Governors called out National Guard troops at least twenty-four times to quell unrest. The potential for chaos became clear on May 8, when pro-war construction workers beat up anti-war demonstrators in New York City. "It was something I'd never seen before and never seen since," one antiwar activist said of the mood in New York. "I could feel the polarization."[15] In Congress, the invasion stirred an uproar. After symbolically chastising Nixon by repealing the 1964 Gulf of Tonkin Resolution, the Senate voted to cut off funds for U.S. operations in Cambodia and to force the withdrawal of U.S. troops from all of Indochina by 1972. The more conservative House of Representatives defeated those efforts, but there was no doubt that liberals would continue to seek ways to constrain Nixon's ability to continue the war.

Exhausted and often alcohol-fogged, Nixon lashed back furiously at his critics. He denigrated antiwar activists as "bums" and privately blasted liberals in Congress and the media. "They hate us, the country, themselves, their wives, everything they do—these liberals," the president snarled.[16] Desperate to crack down, he approved a proposal to allow federal agents to spy on antiwar activists by opening mail, carrying out burglaries, and conducting electronic surveillance. The FBI vetoed the draconian scheme, but Nixon's preferences for bold action against the antiwar movement were clear. Intelligence agencies, the Justice Department, and the Internal Revenue Service stepped up harassment of activists, whom the president increasingly regarded as personal enemies.

These abuses prefigured the 1972 Watergate burglary that would ultimately destroy the Nixon presidency. In the short term, however, Nixon succeeded in defying his adversaries. Congress was not yet ready to force his hand, and the antiwar movement, already deeply factionalized, lost momentum once American troops withdrew from Cambodia in late June. The White House could draw encouragement as well from opinion polls showing strong

'CHOPPING BLOCK'

A cartoon published on May 7, 1970, suggests the impact of the Vietnam War on American society. (Newsday)

disapproval of antiwar agitation and surprisingly high approval—59 percent on June 2—for the administration. In the November 1970 elections, the Republicans fared well, losing nine seats in the House but gaining two in the Senate. Encouraged, Nixon pressed on with his Vietnam policy, still searching for the formula that would bring success.

THE TURN

Despite all its efforts, the Nixon administration failed to turn the situation to its advantage. While Hanoi refused as adamantly as ever to alter its peace terms, the South Vietnamese state remained fragile. Even Saigon's alleged achievements during the early

1970s were questionable at best. Pacification depended on torture, assassination, and forced relocation, which may have done as much to alienate peasants from the government as to draw them closer. Nor was the land reform effective. Demand for land—and thus the political payoff for redistributing it—declined sharply as farmers flooded to the cities, reducing the peasantry from 80 percent of the South Vietnamese population in 1961 to 70 percent ten years later. Nation-building efforts that might have yielded results in earlier decades were, by the 1970s, too little, too late.[17] The ARVN, meanwhile, continued to suffer from corruption, desertion, and poor leadership, while its battlefield successes probably owed much to deliberate decisions by Hanoi to pull back into a defensive mode and await U.S. withdrawals.

These underlying problems manifested themselves in two dramatic events that helped convince the Nixon administration that it could not win the sort of settlement it wanted. In February 1971, ARVN units fought poorly during an invasion of Laos designed to destroy communist bases and a critical section of the Ho Chi Minh Trail. The operation, conducted without American ground troops, confirmed fears among many U.S. officials that the ARVN stood little chance of holding its own against North Vietnamese troops. National elections in October showed Nguyen Van Thieu was doing little better in the political realm. Thieu won a new presidential term with 94.3 percent of the vote, but it was common knowledge that his victory was a result of massive fraud and manipulation.

New domestic troubles also weighed on Nixon during 1971. The Laos fiasco broke "the thin thread" of public faith in the administration's Vietnam policy, he lamented.[18] Scarcely was that episode over when shocking revelations about the conduct of the war compounded the administration's problems. First, the nation was riveted by a war crimes trial that raised questions about the morality of U.S. policy. Accused of murder for his part in a

*South Vietnamese troops ride a U.S.-supplied armored vehicle along the
Ho Chi Minh Trail during the invasion of Laos in 1971. (Douglas Pike
Collection, Vietnam Archive, Texas Tech University, VA002286)*

massacre of more than three hundred civilians at the hamlet of
My Lai, Army Lt. William Calley described savage combat conditions in which American soldiers viewed all Vietnamese as the
enemy. Next, sensational media reports gave Americans new
reason to doubt their elected leaders. On June 13, 1971, the *New
York Times* began publishing excerpts of a top-secret Defense
Department study that revealed, among other instances of presidential dishonesty, Lyndon Johnson's failure to inform Americans of his decisions to take the country to war in 1964 and 1965.
Nixon lashed out at Daniel Ellsberg, the former government official responsible for the leak, and appealed to the Supreme Court
to bar further publication of the so-called Pentagon Papers. In a
landmark victory for press freedom, however, the court rebuffed

Nixon, permitting Americans to read at length about the questionable decision making that had led to war.

Stark evidence of discontent within the U.S. military also fed mounting national pessimism. Disgruntled veterans increasingly spoke out, most strikingly when two thousand members of Vietnam Veterans Against the War staged a four-day "invasion" of Washington in April 1971. Former soldiers in ragged military uniforms symbolically rejected the medals they had won in Vietnam, hurling them onto the steps of the U.S. Capitol. At a Senate hearing, John Kerry, a Navy veteran who later pursued a career in politics, called the war "the biggest nothing in history" and asked, "How do you ask a man to be the last man to die for a mistake?"[19]

Many soldiers in South Vietnam were posing the same question. Discipline and morale plummeted as the U.S. force dwindled toward one hundred fifty thousand soldiers by the end of 1971. Drug use became widespread, and soldiers sometimes refused dangerous missions. The number of reported "fraggings"—attacks by enlisted men against officers, often using fragmentation grenades—swelled to 271 in 1970 and 333 in 1971. "By every conceivable indicator," wrote Robert Heinl, a retired officer who studied U.S. forces in 1971, "our army that now remains in Vietnam is in a state of approaching collapse, with individual units avoiding or having refused combat, murdering their officers and noncommissioned officers, drug-ridden and dispirited where not near-mutinous."[20]

All these developments altered the U.S. political landscape in ways Nixon could not ignore. More and more Americans, including many who reviled the antiwar movement, became convinced that the war was taking too heavy a toll and must be ended. According to a poll taken just after Calley's conviction for murder, 58 percent of Americans believed it was "morally wrong" for the United States to be fighting in Vietnam, while only 29 percent disagreed. Meanwhile, Americans indicated, 60 percent to 26 percent, that they favored withdrawal of American troops even if it led to the collapse of South Vietnam.[21]

Anxious about his prospects for reelection in 1972, Nixon began to adjust the American negotiating position. Using the secret channel to Hanoi, Kissinger offered a major concession in May 1971. The United States, he declared, would withdraw all its troops from South Vietnam without requiring a simultaneous pullout by North Vietnamese forces. For the first time, that is, Washington acknowledged that it could not dislodge North Vietnamese power from the South. Nixon and Kissinger still hoped that Vietnamization would ensure the survival of South Vietnam. But the concession reflected a realization that they might have to settle for what Kissinger called a "decent interval" solution to the war.[22] Under this scenario, Washington would settle for a peace deal that assured a sufficient time lag between the removal of U.S. troops and a communist takeover to enable the administration to avoid the appearance of responsibility for South Vietnam's collapse. In this way, Nixon could claim to have achieved "peace with honor" and to have protected U.S. credibility.

The concession produced by far the most serious bargaining since negotiations had opened three years earlier. When Hanoi gratified Washington by promising to release all U.S. prisoners of war as soon as the last American troops withdrew, only one major sticking point remained—the status of Nguyen Van Thieu's regime in Saigon. North Vietnamese negotiators insisted on Thieu's removal from power. Nixon, fearful that ousting Thieu might mean the quick collapse of South Vietnam, refused to abandon his ally. The talks stalled over this issue in September 1971.

The breakdown convinced North Vietnamese leaders that new military efforts would be needed to force further American concessions. By the end of the year, planning was under way for a major offensive. Weakness of the NLF continued to worry

Hanoi, but communist officials believed they had a solution—unprecedentedly bold attacks by large units of North Vietnamese regulars. The delivery of Soviet tanks and other advanced weapons emboldened Hanoi to take this approach, as did the continued withdrawal of U.S. forces, which drastically lessened the chance that a major offensive would be defeated. With only about ninety-five thousand U.S. personnel remaining (including a mere six thousand combat-ready troops), the North Vietnamese communist party approved a massive attack aimed at producing a "fundamental change in the battlefield situation," exposing ARVN weaknesses, and heightening pressure on Nixon before the November 1972 election.[23]

North Vietnamese leaders also had diplomatic considerations in mind as they planned to retake the initiative. By the early 1970s, Hanoi increasingly feared that the Soviet Union and China might, precisely as Washington hoped, begin to press for peace in Vietnam in order to advance the relaxation of superpower relations that both had begun eagerly pursuing with the United States. As yet, there was no immediate reason for panic. More anxious than ever about losing face in the Sino-Soviet struggle for leadership of the communist bloc, both Moscow and Beijing continued to send large quantities of aid. But North Vietnamese leaders worried that the communist powers might soon reorder their priorities, abandoning Hanoi in favor of better relations with Washington. As in 1968, they reasoned that a major offensive would make clear their determination to fight on to victory.

PEACE OF A SORT

The three-pronged Nguyen Hue Offensive, known in the West as the Easter Offensive, opened on March 30, 1972, when North Vietnamese troops burst across the seventeenth parallel into the northernmost provinces of South Vietnam. In the following days, separate forces struck from bases in Cambodia and Laos toward Saigon and into the Central Highlands. Using mass assaults backed by Soviet-made tanks and artillery, the attackers, numbering one hundred twenty-two thousand in all, scored quick successes. On the northern front, North Vietnamese troops overran Quang Tri province, sending thousands of refugees streaming south. The attack into the Highlands threatened to split South Vietnam in two, while the drive toward Saigon enabled communist troops to occupy large areas along the Cambodian border. All over South Vietnam, meanwhile, NLF activities sprang back to life as ARVN troops abandoned pacification duties to fight the invasion.

The strength of the onslaught shocked Nixon, who decided to act boldly to prevent it from toppling the Saigon regime. The president worried that defeat would imperil his reelection, but he and Kissinger also saw grander interests at stake. By early 1972, the administration was making bold strides to implement its long-cherished plan for a more cooperative and stable global order rooted in a balance of power among the United States, the Soviet Union, and China. Nixon had just returned from a landmark trip to Beijing—the first step, Nixon hoped, toward the establishment of full U.S.–Chinese relations—and planned to visit Moscow later in the year to sign a major arms-control treaty. With superpower relations in this promising but delicate state, Nixon and Kissinger feared that a humiliating defeat for the United States would damage the blossoming détente by weakening the American bargaining position and damaging American prestige worldwide.

Vowing not to permit a "little shit-ass country" to defeat his bid for historic breakthroughs, Nixon ordered massive air strikes.[24] "The bastards have never been bombed like they're going to be bombed this time," he growled.[25] Implementing parts of the old Duck Hook plan, Nixon launched round-the-clock raids on North Vietnam—the first such attacks since October 1968—and against advancing communist troops in the South. In May, he went further by ordering the mining of Haiphong harbor. Nixon aimed not only to defeat the offensive but also to gain concessions at the bargaining table. Once more, he tried for a decisive blow that would end the war on his terms.

In some ways, the American onslaught, code-named Linebacker, was a success for Nixon. Bombing inflicted heavy losses, blunted the offensive by early May, and enabled ARVN forces to retake lost territory in some places. Moreover, the bombings bolstered Nixon's approval ratings. Antiwar activism flared briefly, but on the whole Americans viewed the U.S. air campaign as a justifiable response to aggression. Best of all for Nixon, the U.S. counterattack did not derail his diplomatic initiatives with Moscow and Beijing. To the contrary, Soviet and Chinese leaders worried as much as their U.S. counterparts that the surge of fighting would harm the new spirit of détente and, in a major turnabout feared in Hanoi, secretly urged North Vietnam to end the war. At long last, Nixon's effort to drive a wedge between Hanoi and its communist patrons was succeeding.

The bombing did not, however, shift the momentum of the war back in Washington's favor. When the fighting dwindled in September, communist troops occupied new swaths of territory and operated more freely in the South than they had in years, renewing optimism among sympathetic villagers. "In general, the people's morale rose very high thanks to the presence of the North Vietnamese troops," recalled one NLF operative.[26] Among less committed parts of the population, meanwhile, war-weariness intensified. But the most promising development for Hanoi was mounting evidence that the ARVN could not resist North Vietnamese forces unless strongly backed by American air power.

Nor did the shifting Soviet and Chinese positions amount to a major setback for Hanoi. Neither superpower, after all, had urged North Vietnam to concede defeat. Rather, Moscow and Beijing

North Vietnamese soldiers operate an antiaircraft gun near Hanoi on May 23, 1972, during U.S. bombing raids intended to punish North Vietnam for the Easter Offensive. (Douglas Pike Collection, Vietnam Archive, Texas Tech University, VA003828)

counseled Hanoi merely to defer victory by reaching a peace deal that would remove American forces. North Vietnam could then seek opportunities later to defeat South Vietnam and achieve reunification. Though surely resentful of Soviet and Chinese pressure, North Vietnamese officials, horrified by the destructiveness of American bombing but confident of their chances against the ARVN, were no doubt thinking along the same lines. Since Nixon and Kissinger had already acknowledged in 1971 that they might do no better than a "decent interval" solution, the makings of a peace settlement were falling into place.

Negotiators made rapid progress when talks resumed in mid-July 1972. Chief North Vietnamese negotiator Le Duc Tho made the crucial concession, abandoning Hanoi's long-standing demand for the removal of Thieu. Instead, he proposed allowing the existing Saigon government to participate alongside the communist-dominated Provisional Revolutionary Government and neutralist elements in a tripartite commission that would supervise postwar elections and implement other peace provisions. The new body, Le Duc Tho conceded, would make decisions only by unanimity, meaning that Thieu would have veto power. Kissinger readily accepted the plan, even though it meant abandoning his once iron-clad commitment to the Saigon regime. In the best case, he and Nixon believed, continued American aid would enable Thieu to hold his ground. In the worst case, the communists would defeat him—but not right away.

By early fall, Kissinger and Le Duc Tho had worked out a deal. Within sixty days of a cease-fire, the United States would withdraw all remaining troops in South Vietnam, and Hanoi would return American POWs. The tripartite organization, known as the National Council of Reconciliation and Concord, would then take charge of resolving the future of South Vietnam. On October 11, Kissinger left Paris in an exuberant mood, planning to travel to Hanoi eleven days later to sign the accord.

But the deal quickly disintegrated. Angered by Kissinger's failure to consult closely with him during the talks, Nguyen Van Thieu bitterly rejected the deal, protesting that he was no mere "lackey of the U.S."[27] Thieu especially attacked the provisions permitting North Vietnamese troops to remain in South Vietnam and allowing the communists a role in determining the nation's future. All in all, Thieu insisted, it would be better to keep fighting than to accept such a deal. Kissinger spurned this last-minute challenge and urged Nixon to sign the accord without Thieu's approval. Desperate to keep the deal alive, Kissinger told journalists on October 26 that "peace is at hand."[28]

Peace was still some weeks off, however, for Nixon sided with Thieu. Sympathetic to South Vietnamese complaints and emboldened by his landslide reelection on November 7, Nixon decided to reopen key provisions of the accord. In Paris, North Vietnamese negotiators objected vehemently, accusing Kissinger of double-crossing them. Kissinger privately berated Le Duc Tho and his aides as "just a bunch of shits."[29] With renewed talks going nowhere, Nixon opted once again for military coercion. On December 18, 1972, he unleashed a new aerial onslaught aimed at intimidating Hanoi and reassuring Saigon that the United States would not abandon South Vietnam. Over the next eleven days, U.S. B-52s dropped thirty-six thousand tons of bombs— more than the total tonnage dropped from 1969 to 1971—on military sites and densely populated civilian areas throughout North Vietnam.

One day after sustaining the most intense day of aerial bombardment in world history, the Hanoi government announced on December 27 that it was prepared to reopen the Paris negotiations. By January 9, the two sides were moving rapidly toward an agreement. Yet the "Christmas bombing," as American commentators dubbed the campaign, was hardly a success. Hanoi, eager to end the American war, unquestionably would have resumed talks without the attacks. Meanwhile, the bombing stirred vociferous condemnation in Congress and around the world, with Swedish Prime Minister Olaf Palme comparing U.S. actions to the Nazi Holocaust. At the same time, the attacks failed to reassure Thieu, who remained deeply suspicious of American abandonment. But the starkest evidence of failure was the simple fact that the peace deal signed on January 27, 1973, differed only cosmetically from the accord hammered out in October. Fearful of congressional action to force an end to the war, Nixon accepted virtually the same terms he had previously rejected, and this time he made clear to the Saigon government that it had no choice but to accept. He sweetened the deal for Thieu only by personally assuring him that the United States would reenter the war with "full force" if Hanoi violated the agreement.[30]

Nixon declared he had achieved the "peace with honor" that he had promised when taking office four years earlier.[31] South Vietnam still stood, Thieu remained in office, and enormous quantities of American economic and military aid continued to flow to the Saigon government. But the future of South Vietnam, along with that of Cambodia and Laos, was anything but certain. The peace accord spelled out provisions by which the NLF might gain significant influence by peaceful means. Much more menacing, some one hundred fifty thousand North Vietnamese troops remained in South Vietnam. Just as in 1954, the peace accord meant that foreign forces could go home, but it resolved little else.

WARS UNENDING

THE 1973 PEACE ACCORD, BLANDLY TITLED THE "Agreement on Ending the War and Restoring Peace in Vietnam," inspired little celebration. "This is not like the end of World War II," lamented Captain Herbert Carter, a twenty-nine-year-old helicopter pilot based near Saigon when the fighting ended. "We didn't win a war. There's nothing clear-cut. Nobody surrendered."[1] A similar sense of inconclusiveness prevailed among South Vietnamese of all political stripes. The only certainty seemed to be more hardship ahead.

Pessimism proved well justified. As the last American troops departed, a brutal new phase of the war opened. Renewed combat between South Vietnamese and communist forces reflected the fact that the peace agreement, much like the Geneva Accords two decades earlier, did little to resolve the basic causes of conflict. The destiny of the South still hung in the balance, and neither Saigon nor Hanoi was willing to compromise. It would take another two years of hard fighting to settle the matter finally in the communists' favor.

Suffering, turmoil, and controversy lingered long after the final burst of combat. Northern control over all Vietnam brought stiff punishment for many Southerners. Meanwhile the whole population endured enormous hardship as Hanoi imposed communism in the South and undertook new military campaigns. Much greater horrors unfolded in Laos and especially Cambodia. For Americans, the war left not only physical scars but also deep social cleavages and pervasive anxiety about national decline. Even in the twenty-first century, painful memories of the Vietnam War weighed heavily on Americans and Southeast Asians alike.

THE CEASE-FIRE WAR

Washington and Hanoi quickly implemented the parts of the Paris agreements laying out procedures for U.S. withdrawal. North Vietnam released all 591 U.S. servicemen it held as prisoners of war. The POWs, who had endured as much as eight years of sometimes brutal captivity, returned to patriotic fanfare in the United States. The last few thousand U.S. troops in South Vietnam went home as well, usually to much cooler receptions. By the end of March 1973, only a small detachment of Marines remained to guard the U.S. Embassy in Saigon.

None of the signatories showed much interest, however, in carrying out treaty provisions for a political settlement in South Vietnam. The Saigon government, which had the most to lose through enforcement of the agreement, made clear it would not cooperate with the Provisional Revolutionary Government, the body established by the NLF in 1969. President Nguyen Van Thieu clung to his policy of the "four no's": no negotiations with the communists, no surrender of territory, no coalition government, and no communist political activity. Meanwhile, Saigon violated the cease-fire by launching attacks to extend its control into areas dominated by the communists. In part, these attacks reflected confidence. Saigon controlled about 75 percent of South Vietnamese territory at the time of the Paris agreement and held big advantages in troops and matériel thanks to huge deliveries of American aid. But Southern militancy also sprang from anxiety. Despite Nixon's assurances of U.S. support, Thieu suspected that Washington, tired of the war and consumed by domestic problems, would lose interest before long. South Vietnam, Thieu calculated, had to act boldly while it could still count on Washington's backing.

Hanoi had a similarly complicated view. On the one hand, communist leaders saw little prospect that Saigon would go along with the Paris accords and geared up for more fighting. North Vietnam reequipped its forces below the seventeenth parallel and modernized its supply network, notably by constructing an oil pipeline and a network of paved roads into the South. On the other hand, the communists saw reasons to avoid bold moves in the near term. North Vietnamese and NLF forces needed time to recover their strength after heavy fighting in 1972. In addition, communist leaders feared that dramatic military action might provoke the United States to reenter the war. Although communist troops frequently violated the cease-fire, they limited themselves to small-scale operations designed to consolidate authority in areas controlled by the Provisional Revolutionary Government. Otherwise, the communists concentrated on political agitation against Thieu.

Rapid intensification of South Vietnamese military activities in late 1973 altered Hanoi's calculations. Some North Vietnamese leaders continued to advocate caution. As in past debates, however, hawks soon gained the upper hand. These officials believed that communist forces, though outnumbered in the South by as much as four to one, held decisive advantages in morale and organization. This view prevailed in October 1973 at a meeting of communist leaders held in Hanoi. Under "Resolution 21," the party decreed that prospects for revolution in South Vietnam were better than at any time since 1954 and called for "continuous revolutionary violence" to overthrow the Saigon regime.[2]

More aggressive operations brought results that exceeded Hanoi's highest hopes. In late 1973 and early 1974, North Vietnamese and NLF attackers mauled ARVN forces in several areas, retaking former communist strongholds and demolishing Saigon's pacification efforts. Optimism spread rapidly among communist leaders, especially as it became clear that they had little to fear from the United States. Precisely as Hanoi hoped—and Thieu dreaded—Washington steadily distanced itself from Vietnam following the Paris agreement.

At first after the accord, Nixon had acted boldly to defend his ally. He handed over vast quantities of military hardware and skirted the peace terms by categorizing U.S. military personnel as civilian advisers to the Saigon regime. "You can be sure that we stand with you," the president told Thieu.[3] Meanwhile, Nixon continued the U.S. bombing of Cambodia, where the Khmer Rouge was steadily gaining ground. As the months passed, however, Nixon encountered mounting obstacles to these efforts. Weary of war, clear majorities of Congress and the American public wanted to end U.S. involvement in Southeast Asia once and for all. Pervasive skepticism about the president's Indochina policies grew into outright rebellion as the Watergate scandal escalated in 1973. With evidence piling up about the 1972 break-in at Democratic Party headquarters and Nixon's attempts to hinder investigators, everything the president stood for—not least his commitment to South Vietnam—seemed tainted by cynicism and abuse of power.

Congress repeatedly flexed its muscles to constrain the president. First, it forced Nixon to agree to end all military operations in Indochina by August 15, 1973. It then passed the War Powers Act, which created barriers to future use of American forces. Under the measure, the president had to inform Congress within forty-eight hours of any deployment of American troops anywhere in the world and to withdraw them from hostilities within sixty days unless Congress approved. Finally, Congress reined in U.S. spending on South Vietnam. In August 1974, legislators approved just $750 million in military and economic assistance, half of the $1.5 billion desired by the White House and less than a third of the $2.3 billion Washington had spent on military aid alone in 1973.

The cutback dealt a psychological blow to Saigon and hampered South Vietnamese military operations by creating shortages of fuel and equipment. But declining American support was hardly the only problem confronting Saigon. The government's gravest weakness remained what it had always been—an inability to build effective national institutions supported by the population. Despite Vietnamization, the ARVN continued to suffer from rampant desertion and poor morale. Meanwhile, Saigon's economic failings became more glaring than ever. For years, the United States had sustained South Vietnam by flooding the country with consumer goods and directly or indirectly employing hundreds of thousands of Vietnamese as everything from clerks to taxi drivers to prostitutes. The U.S. withdrawal left behind unemployment, inflation, and a stunted manufacturing sector. South Vietnamese cities seethed with discontent on a scale not seen in years. As always, however, Saigon's problems were most severe in the countryside. The extent of territory controlled by the ARVN masked hatred among many peasants for the corruption and brutality they associated with South Vietnamese leaders. "We now understand what it is like under the Government of the Republic of Vietnam," asserted one peasant from an ARVN-dominated village near Hue. "For the poor people of Vietnam, could it be any worse under the Liberation side?"[4]

All these problems coalesced to bring about the collapse of South Vietnam. The final phase began on August 9, 1974, when

Nixon resigned the presidency. Overnight, Hanoi no longer had to worry about the American leader who had done most to assure Saigon of U.S. support. To test the intentions of the new president, Gerald Ford, North Vietnam launched a major attack northeast of Saigon in December. The operation brought doubly good news for the communists. The entire province of Phuoc Long fell to the communists, while Ford, hemmed in by Congress and wary of embroiling his presidency in Vietnam, did nothing. Emboldened North Vietnamese leaders drafted a two-stage plan for bold offensives in 1975, followed in 1976 by the "victorious conclusion of the war."[5]

Total victory came much more quickly than anticipated. In mid-March, communist troops captured the strategically important city of Ban Me Thuot in the Central Highlands. Further communist advances led Thieu to order ARVN forces to evacuate the Central Highlands altogether. The chaotic withdrawal left six provinces in communist hands and obliterated any remaining confidence in Thieu's leadership. By April 1, the stunning rout had spread to the coast. Hue, Da Nang, and other cities fell to the communists, sometimes without a fight. Astonished by the rapidity of their advance, North Vietnamese commanders hurriedly turned their attention to capturing Saigon.

With South Vietnam in mortal danger, Ford asked Congress for $722 million in emergency military aid. But most Americans—Ford included—saw no hope of rescuing the country. The request partly reflected the administration's fear of damaging American credibility if it did nothing. It also stemmed from a cynical desire to pin the blame for Saigon's final collapse on Congress, which Ford knew was certain to reject the request. Indeed, Congress, unwilling to pump more money into a losing cause, quickly blocked the proposal, approving instead $300 million to pay for humanitarian relief and the evacuation of Americans from South

A North Vietnamese T-54 tank, supplied by the Soviet Union, crashes through the gates of the Presidential Palace in Saigon on April 30, 1975. (AFP/Getty Images)

Vietnam. Out of options, Ford declared on April 23 that the Vietnam War was "finished as far as America is concerned."[6]

Yet a final series of indignities remained for the United States over the following days. Thieu resigned the presidency of South Vietnam and castigated Washington as "irresponsible" and "inhumane" for failing to honor its promises of support.[7] A few days later, U.S. troops began Operation Frequent Wind, the evacuation of American personnel and of South Vietnamese who had worked closely with the United States. The process degenerated into a humiliating spectacle of defeat as U.S. soldiers grappled with South Vietnamese mobs desperately seeking space on the last helicopters headed for U.S. warships waiting off the coast. A few hours after the final chopper lifted off the roof of a building near the U.S. Embassy, a North Vietnamese tank smashed through the gates of the presidential palace in central Saigon. A soldier raced to the top floor and ran the colors of the National Liberation Front up the flagpole. The American war was over.

NATIONS IN TORMENT

Communist propaganda promised that the end of the war would bring harmony and prosperity to Vietnam. "The path on which we are advancing is clear and our future is very bright," the party declared.[8] The reality was different. Although estimates vary, some historians claim that the communists executed as many as sixty-five thousand Southerners.[9] The regime sent at least two hundred thousand more to reeducation camps—prisons ostensibly for rehabilitating foes of communism—for several years and a much larger number for shorter periods.[10] Other Southerners were pushed to the margins of society by bans on employment or forced relocation to remote areas. Even Southerners who had backed the NLF sometimes fared badly. For years, Hanoi had proclaimed its respect for the NLF as a separate entity and pledged that reunification would come about through negotiation once the war was won. In the end, North Vietnam simply imposed its rule on the South, permitting Southern revolutionaries scant role in governing the unified Socialist Republic of Vietnam after it was formally established on July 2, 1976. Despite the joys of national reunification, bitterness ran just beneath the surface.

Throughout the country, Vietnamese endured grinding poverty. The crisis stemmed partly from catastrophic damage caused by the war. Besides killing between two million and three million Vietnamese from 1960 to 1975 and maiming roughly the same number, fighting had destroyed millions of acres of farmland, pulverized the country's industrial facilities, and damaged many villages and cities. Foreign aid, meanwhile, was in short supply. Communist leaders insisted that the United States deliver $3.25 billion in reconstruction aid that Nixon had tentatively promised as part of the 1973 Paris agreement, but few Americans had any interest in following through. Hanoi compounded its woes in 1978 by abruptly attempting to force a socialist transformation in the south. Collectivization of agriculture exacerbated food shortages and, along with another law abolishing private commerce, stirred bitter resentment against the government. As many as a million people, including a large number of ethnic Chinese who had long been a cornerstone of the economy, fled the country, often in rickety boats. Many of these "boat people" endured horrific voyages and squalid refugee camps before finding permanent homes in the United States or elsewhere.

None of this came close, however, to the stunning brutality in Cambodia. The country's five-year-old civil war ended on April 17, 1975, when the communist Khmer Rouge captured the capital, Phnom Penh. The Nixon administration had gone to extraordinary lengths to prevent that outcome, not least by bombing Cambodia with more explosive power than the United States had used against Japan during all of World War II. But the Khmer Rouge had made steady progress, especially after Congress mandated an end to U.S. involvement in August 1973. Led by a Western-educated zealot known as Pol Pot, the new government declared the "year zero" and set about remaking Cambodian society according to an extreme Maoist vision of agrarian egalitarianism. The Khmer Rouge emptied the cities, imposed forced labor, and killed an estimated two million fellow Cambodians, especially members of ethnic minorities, city dwellers, and educated people.

The end of the Vietnam War also brought grim consequences in Laos. Emboldened by the communist triumphs in Vietnam and Cambodia, the communist Pathet Lao took power in August

1975. For some Laotians, the communist triumph meant relief from years of fighting during which the United States had bombed the country even more intensely than Cambodia. Peace brought tragedy, however, for the Hmong, an ethnic minority group strongly opposed to the communists. Starting in 1961, the Central Intelligence Agency had recruited an army of Hmong tribesmen to attack North Vietnamese and Pathet Lao forces. The communists exacted revenge after taking power. The new Laotian government tracked down and killed as many as one hundred thousand Hmong, and an equal number fled the country.[11]

As these horrors unfolded in Southeast Asia, nightmares of a different type haunted U.S. policymakers in Washington. Would the communist takeovers in Vietnam, Laos, and Cambodia cause other countries to fall to communism like a row of dominoes? Would allies see America's defeat as the start of U.S. retreat from global leadership? Would enemies challenge the United States everywhere? The Ford administration betrayed its anxieties in the first days after the fall of Saigon. Standing in front of a U.S. aircraft carrier, the president declared on May 4, 1975, "We are strong, and we will continue to be strong."[12] A few days later, Ford found occasion to deliver on his pledge. When Khmer Rouge authorities briefly detained the crew of the American cargo ship *Mayaguez* off the Cambodian coast, he ordered a vigorous military strike on Cambodian territory without waiting to see whether the U.S. sailors would be peacefully released.

To a degree, American concern about credibility proved justified. The U.S. defeat in Vietnam emboldened Soviet leaders to challenge U.S. interests in Africa and Central America. Overall, however, the United States suffered remarkably few geopolitical setbacks. Within Indochina, communist victories did not bring the sort of rigid Chinese domination that U.S. policymakers had feared for so many years. In fact, tension between China and Vietnam mounted quickly as the two countries clashed over the future order in Southeast Asia. The bitterest dispute arose over Cambodia, where the pro-Chinese Khmer Rouge persecuted ethnic Vietnamese and launched attacks against Vietnamese border areas. With China backing the Cambodians, the Hanoi regime looked to Moscow for help. Any pretense of communist unity dissolved entirely in early 1979. First, Vietnamese forces invaded Cambodia and overthrew the Khmer Rouge. The Chinese government, seeking to punish Hanoi, then launched a bloody monthlong border war against Vietnam. International communist solidarity, so celebrated just twenty-five years earlier, had broken down completely in the face of fratricidal rivalries among communist nations.

Beyond Indochina, meanwhile, dominoes did not fall. Thailand, Indonesia, and other Southeast Asian nations, fearful of Vietnamese expansion and Soviet influence, remained strongly anticommunist. Nor did defeat in Vietnam cause lasting damage to U.S. interests in the wider world. Washington's alliances survived without serious challenge. Over the long run, the defeat may even have benefited Washington by emboldening Moscow to undertake ventures in the Third World that turned out to be immensely costly and draining. Above all, Soviet intervention in Afghanistan deteriorated into a brutal war that many commentators likened to the U.S. experience in Vietnam.

The Vietnam War had a much more profound effect on America's domestic life. In material terms, massive U.S. spending on the conflict—more than $150 billion—fueled deficits that contributed to a severe economic crisis throughout the 1970s. But the war left its deepest imprint on the attitudes Americans held about their country. In earlier years, most Americans had unquestioningly trusted their leaders and assumed their nation's fundamental benevolence, greatness, and worthiness as a model for other societies. Following the war, Americans were no longer so sure. Opinion polls, reflecting the effect of the Watergate scandal and America's economic woes as well as the war, revealed dramatically lower levels of confidence in the presidency, Congress, and the military. President Jimmy Carter captured the dour mood in 1977, asserting that the United States was suffering a "profound moral crisis" brought on by the "intellectual and moral poverty" that had led the United States to disaster in Vietnam.[13] Prominent commentators such as novelist Tom Wolfe and historian Christopher Lasch criticized Americans for abandoning old values in favor of crass materialism, while California Governor Jerry Brown declared that the United States had entered an "era of limits."[14]

Distrust and doubt manifested themselves in complicated ways during the first years after the war. In 1976, Americans showed a desire to atone for past errors by electing Carter to the presidency. A man of strong moral convictions, Carter appealed to voters largely on the strength of his promises to restore honesty in government and to open a new era of foreign policy emphasizing democratization and respect for human rights. Some Americans showed their distrust of authority by charging that Vietnam, possibly with Washington's connivance, was still holding U.S. servicemen officially categorized as "missing in action." Mostly, though, Americans coped with painful memories by avoiding the bitter controversies that the war had generated. In contrast to the accolades it showered on soldiers returning from other wars, the nation greeted its 2.6 million Vietnam veterans with stony indifference and sometimes mocked them as drug-addled, violence-prone misfits. The experience embittered former servicemen and left many of those who had been wounded— three hundred seventy thousand with physical injuries and many more with a psychological ailment known as Post-Traumatic Stress Disorder—to suffer in obscurity. Meanwhile, the war generated remarkably little public debate about its origins, outcome, and meaning for the nation's future.

CONTESTED LEGACIES

The Vietnam War reemerged in the late 1970s as a major topic of discussion among Americans. It did so partly because sufficient time had passed to ease the immediate exhaustion and demoralization following eight years of war. Partly, too, a dramatic escalation of international tensions in 1979 and 1980 refocused the nation's attention on Vietnam. First, Marxist revolutionaries overthrew the U.S.-supported government of Nicaragua. Then Islamic militants in Iran toppled the U.S.-backed government and seized the staff of the American embassy in Tehran as hostages. Finally, Soviet forces invaded Afghanistan and appeared poised to extend Moscow's influence toward the oil-rich Persian Gulf. For the first time since the fall of Saigon, Americans had to decide how to respond to serious challenges abroad, a dilemma that inevitably led them to reconsider all aspects of the war in Vietnam.

Consensus emerged on a few matters. Breaking abruptly with past ambivalence, Americans across the political spectrum celebrated the courage and selflessness of Vietnam veterans. Congress approved programs aimed at easing the wrenching physical and psychological problems that many of them still confronted. "The nation is ready to change its heart, its mind and its attitude about the men who had fought in the war," asserted Carter as he declared Vietnam Veterans Week in May 1979.[15] As if to prove Carter's point, Americans turned out in huge numbers to visit the national Vietnam Veterans Memorial in Washington, D.C., after it opened in 1982. The centerpiece of the memorial, two imposing marble walls etched with the names of 58,249 American soldiers killed in Vietnam, quickly became one of the capital's most heavily visited attractions, a solemn place that evoked a blend of mourning, tribute, and reconciliation.

On many issues, however, intensifying discussion of the war during the 1980s generated fierce debate. Perhaps the loudest

The Vietnam Veterans Memorial, completed in 1982, stands a short walk from the Washington Monument on the National Mall in Washington, D.C. (Courtesy Marty Baldessari)

disagreement arose over the appropriate U.S. response to challenges abroad. Some Americans invoked Vietnam in arguing that the nation must steer clear of new foreign ventures. But many others supported Ronald Reagan, who, as the Republican nominee for president in 1980, insisted that the United States must reassert its power internationally. As part of his bid to overcome the sense of caution he labeled the "Vietnam syndrome," Reagan boldly challenged the notion that the United States had dishonored itself in Vietnam and must therefore tread lightly in the future. "It's time we recognized that ours was, in truth, a noble cause," Reagan asserted in a campaign speech.[16] Following his landslide election, Reagan undertook a massive military buildup and began sending enormous quantities of supplies to anticommunist forces throughout the Third World.

He went still further in October 1983, sending seven thousand troops to overthrow the Marxist government of the tiny Caribbean nation of Grenada. That operation, the first combat deployment of U.S. forces since the Vietnam War, won broad support among Americans. It did not banish anxieties, however, about the use of U.S. soldiers abroad. On the contrary, the Reagan administration ran into ardent congressional and public opposition when it hinted at the possibility of sending troops to help fight leftist insurgents in El Salvador. Intervention in Central America, argued Reagan's critics, risked sinking the United States into another bloody quagmire. Such protests put the administration on the defensive, especially after terrorists killed 241 U.S. Marines taking part in an ill-defined peacekeeping mission in Lebanon. That disaster spurred Defense Secretary Caspar Weinberger to announce in 1984 that the United States would henceforth send troops into action only if they had clear objectives, enjoyed firm public and congressional support, and used sufficient force to ensure success. Secretary of State George Shultz protested the so-called Weinberger Doctrine, warning that the

United States must not become the "Hamlet of nations, worrying endlessly over whether and how to respond" to provocations abroad.[17] But Weinberger's approach prevailed for years to come—powerful evidence that memories of the Vietnam War could not be overcome as easily as champions of a vigorous foreign policy would have liked.

The clash over American activism abroad was intertwined with an increasingly bitter debate over the reasons for the U.S. defeat in Vietnam. Those Americans wariest of international involvement attributed the U.S. failure to a fundamental mismatch between U.S. goals and the basic desires of the Vietnamese people. The United States, in their view, erred by backing a brutal, despotic, and corrupt South Vietnamese regime that never commanded the support of its own people. Exactly why American policymakers made this mistake was a matter of dispute. Liberals tended to blame cultural myopia for blinding U.S. leaders to the subtleties of Vietnamese society, while more radical commentators contended that selfish economic, geostrategic, or political motives led American policymakers to enter into a partnership they knew to be risky. Conservatives rejected both lines of critique, which raised troubling questions about the basic values and priorities that underpinned U.S. policy in the Cold War. They argued instead that the U.S. failure resulted from far less profound—and wholly avoidable—errors of judgment about how to wage the war. Some blamed military leaders for embracing faulty strategies and tactics. Others charged that timid civilian leaders had squandered America's opportunity for victory by refusing to permit the military to do what was necessary to win. Many also blamed the antiwar movement or the media for undermining the war effort.

This debate became popularized by the mid-1980s in an outpouring of novels, memoirs, and movies about the war. "Vietnam was a sure loser in book publishing seven or eight years ago; now it's a big event," said one Boston-based publisher in 1983.[18] But Hollywood films undoubtedly did the most to shape opinion about the war. Several major releases—notably *The Deer Hunter* (1978), *Apocalypse Now* (1979), *Platoon* (1986), and *Full Metal Jacket* (1987)—depicted the war as a grim exercise in futility. Again and again, these films showed America's cherished political principles and vast technological sophistication to be utterly useless against a determined foe in an alien setting. Another genre of movies, including *Missing in Action* (1984) and the *Rambo* series (1982, 1985, and 1988), sent a different message. These macho action movies showed burly American veterans, betrayed by a spineless and corrupt U.S. government, returning to Indochina to rescue abandoned comrades from communist prison camps and to exact revenge for earlier humiliations. "I did what I had to do to win!" John Rambo declares in the 1982 film. "But somebody wouldn't let us win!"[19]

In Vietnam, meanwhile, the 1980s brought discord not about the war itself so much as about the political and economic order that the communist victory had established. In the first years of the decade, the country's fortunes sank from bad to worse. The economy struggled under the weight of rigid communist ideology, international isolation, and extravagant military spending necessitated in part by Vietnam's draining occupation of Cambodia. Copious Soviet aid brought a modicum of relief but also embittered many Vietnamese by transforming the country into a political, military, and economic satellite of Moscow. Some complained that their leaders had driven out the Americans only to be dominated by the Soviets, whom they derided as "Americans without dollars."[20] Discontent with top leaders in Hanoi rippled not only through the Vietnamese population but also within the communist party. The moment of reckoning came in 1986, when reformers ousted Prime Minister Pham Van Dong and other senior officials who had helped lead the party since its earliest days before the Second World War. Under its "renovation" policy (*doi moi*), the new leadership permitted a degree of free enterprise, opened the country to Western goods, abandoned efforts to collectivize agriculture, and expanded civil liberties, although the communist party retained its monopoly on power.

BEYOND THE COLD WAR

The crumbling of the Soviet Union in the late 1980s further moderated the Hanoi government by eliminating Vietnam's main ideological partner and forcing it to seek trade and assistance in other places. The end of the Cold War also eased American hostility to Vietnam. Since 1975, Washington had refused to carry on economic or diplomatic relations with the country. The Carter administration had briefly entertained normalization of ties in the late 1970s, but that initiative quickly collapsed in the face of persistent hostility. Vietnam rebuffed American demands for help accounting for all of the approximately two thousand five hundred U.S. servicemen listed as "missing in action." Washington refused Vietnamese demands for reparations and antagonized Hanoi by pursuing warm relations with China. U.S.-Vietnamese tensions began to ease only in the late 1980s as Hanoi, anxious to overcome its isolation, ended its occupation of Cambodia and adopted a far more cooperative attitude toward locating the remains of missing Americans. The collapse of the Soviet bloc dramatically accelerated the trend toward reconciliation by altering the political landscape within the United States. As anticommunism cooled, antipathy toward Vietnam slackened, and American businesses agitated for access to a potentially lucrative new market.

A few pockets of American hostility toward Vietnam remained, notably among organizations dedicated to the MIA issue and within Vietnamese-American communities strongly critical of the

A woman walks through a new commercial district of Hanoi in January 1994, a few days before the United States formally ended its nineteen-year-old economic embargo against Vietnam. (AP Images/Olivier Nilsson)

communist regime in Hanoi. Nevertheless, normalization of U.S.–Vietnamese relations proceeded. In 1994, Washington lifted its economic embargo. A year later, the United States and Vietnam established full diplomatic ties and began the process of opening embassies. Finally, the two nations signed a trade agreement in 2000. These steps brought rapid political and economic results. Politically, the two governments expressed determination to seek cooperation in areas of mutual concern. Warming relations culminated in November 2000, when President Bill Clinton visited Hanoi and proclaimed the dawn of a new era. "Finally," he declared in a speech to Vietnamese university students, "America is coming to see Vietnam as your people have asked for years—as a country, not a war."[21] Economically, the value of trade between the two countries mushroomed to about $1 billion annually by the turn of the century, and the United States climbed to eighth among foreign investors in Vietnam.

Normalization of relations with Vietnam was just one of many indications that Americans were letting go of old passions surrounding the war. Voters elected Clinton and later George W. Bush to the presidency despite controversy over their successful efforts during the Vietnam era to avoid the draft. Historians increasingly endeavored to set aside old polemics and to analyze the war in all its complexity. Filmmakers also eschewed political controversy, producing a new generation of war movies focused narrowly on the courage of individual soldiers. For politically relevant history, Americans preferred uplifting tales of the "founding fathers" of 1776 or of the "greatest generation" that fought the Second World War—topics that meshed well with the triumphal mood in the United States following its victory in the Cold War.

Even in making foreign policy, the area where memories of Vietnam loomed largest, Americans showed diminished interest in the war during the 1990s. Formally, the U.S. military remained committed to the Weinberger Doctrine, renamed the Powell Doctrine in recognition of the ardor with which General Colin Powell, the chairman of the Joint Chiefs of Staff from 1989 to 1993, urged caution in the use of troops abroad. But Washington grew decidedly bolder in employing force internationally. Americans drew encouragement above all from success in the 1991 Persian Gulf War, the conflict between Iraq and a U.S.-led coalition of nations over the independence of Kuwait. The victory restored the image of the American military and made plain that Washington was capable of using force to crushing effect. "By God, we've kicked the Vietnam syndrome once and for all," declared a jubilant President George H. W. Bush after the fighting ended.[22] Bush overstated his case, for critics of American interventionism continued to invoke Vietnam over the following years. He was, however, on to something. Over the remainder of the 1990s, U.S. leaders sent troops on complex military and political missions to Somalia and Bosnia and undertook a major bombing campaign against Kosovo.

Bush's claim came closest to the mark in the months following the terrorist attacks against New York and Washington on September 11, 2001, when his son George W. Bush held the presidency. To a degree unprecedented since before the Vietnam War, Americans united around a shared sense of national purpose, placed confidence in their leaders, and enjoyed global sympathy. Moreover, they readily backed a major military campaign against Afghanistan, which harbored the terrorists responsible for the 9/11 attacks, despite awareness that the operation posed steep military challenges and might carry indefinite nation-building obligations. Few Americans complained that the United States might be getting itself into another Vietnam War.

Ironically, events that seemed to signal the start of a true post-Vietnam era in the United States led to a powerful resurgence of Vietnam-related controversy. Passions were, it turned out, more dormant than vanquished, liable to spring back to the fore under the right conditions. The catalyst was the U.S. invasion of Iraq in 2003, an ill-advised campaign designed by hawkish policymakers within the George W. Bush administration who believed they could exploit the popularity of U.S. action against Islamic terrorists to overthrow Iraqi leader Saddam Hussein and instigate a political transformation in the Middle East. These "neoconservatives" had argued for years that the United States needed to act boldly in the international arena. The September 11 attacks gave them their opportunity, and they chose to begin with Iraq, long a source of irritation to Washington.

The initial U.S. invasion was a great success, toppling the Baghdad government in about three weeks. A few months later, however, American occupation troops found themselves embroiled in a counterinsurgency war that reminded many observers of Vietnam. Critics of U.S. policy charged that a duplicitous government was once again asking American troops to fight on behalf of a faraway government with little legitimacy among its own people. Bush and his supporters saw a different parallel between Iraq and Vietnam. They contended that antiwar critics, just as in the 1960s and 1970s, were sapping the nation's determination and emboldening its enemies. The United States must not, they insisted, repeat its earlier mistake by withdrawing from Iraq before achieving its objectives.

This debate centered on U.S. foreign and military policy, but it reverberated throughout American society with a power that made it difficult to believe that the Vietnam War would disappear from public debate for many years to come. Deeply unpopular and wildly controversial, the Iraq war posed profoundly divisive social and political questions more forcefully than any event since the Vietnam era. What duty do citizens have toward a government they oppose? What steps can government legitimately take to quash dissent? Can Americans reasonably oppose their government without betraying the troops risking death to carry out that government's policies? What, in short, is the proper relationship between American citizens and government authority? Conservatives viewed the U.S. defeat in Vietnam as a warning about the risks of permissiveness and social fragmentation they associated with the 1960s. Liberals saw the defeat, meanwhile, as evidence of the dangers flowing from hubris among government leaders and excessive deference to authority among the general population. The clash over the meaning of the war reached a crescendo during the 2004 presidential race, when the Democratic nominee, Vietnam veteran John Kerry of Massachusetts, came under withering attack for having spoken out against the war in the early 1970s.

Overt and rancorous controversy in the United States contrasted with generally muted discussion of the war in Vietnam. This dearth of debate resulted partly from the sheer scale of the social and economic transformation that took place in Vietnam starting in the late 1980s. Rapid population growth meant that the vast majority of Vietnamese by the turn of the century was too young to remember the war. Meanwhile, explosive economic change remade Vietnam into a bustling commercial nation facing challenges far different from those of the 1960s or 1970s. Unquestionably, Vietnam remained an impoverished society, ranking 109th among 177 countries surveyed in a 2006 study of living standards around the world.[23] Yet Vietnam's integration into the global economy, culminating in accession to the World Trade Organization in 2007, powerfully invigorated an economy increasingly oriented toward capitalism. The nation nearly doubled its gross domestic product between 2000 and 2005 and achieved annual growth rates second only to China among Asian countries. Many Vietnamese enjoyed unprecedented prosperity even as their society confronted widening disparities of wealth, worsening environmental damage, and other problems of a rapidly modernizing capitalist society.

The lack of forthright discussion of the war also resulted from the Vietnamese government's intolerance of free expression. The communist party's willingness to relax its grip in the economic arena did not carry over into the political or ideological spheres. Not least among the regime's concerns was to buttress its legitimacy by affirming a version of history that celebrated past communist accomplishments, particularly the victories over France and the United States. Government declarations and publications rationalized the monumental bloodshed suffered after 1945 as a necessary price to achieve the sacred goals of national unification and independence. Dissenters risked arrest and imprisonment for expressing critical opinions.

Out of public view, however, the war remained a source of bitterness for many Vietnamese. Millions mourned family members killed in the fighting or searched in vain for the remains of loved ones whose bodies were never recovered. Anguish over the MIA problem weighed heavily over Vietnamese society not only because of the huge number of unrecovered bodies—more than three hundred thousand by the Hanoi government's estimate— but also because of the extraordinary importance many Vietnamese attach to worshipping the remains of deceased relatives. Meanwhile, an estimated one million Vietnamese suffered birth defects and illnesses likely attributable to the use of Agent Orange and other herbicides by U.S. forces. Another culprit— land mines and other unexploded ordnance left over from the war—killed or maimed hundreds of Vietnamese, Cambodians, and Laotians every year even a quarter century after the fighting ended.

But such painful consequences do not encapsulate Vietnamese attitudes toward the war any more than the government's mono-chromatically heroic version of history. Just as in the United States, different Vietnamese people experienced—and remember—the war in markedly different ways. Some faithfully celebrate the

American war as a stirring accomplishment. Others undoubtedly agree with the Vietnamese author and dissident Duong Thu Huong, whose 1988 novel *Paradise of the Blind* berates the communist party for undertaking what she regards as an unnecessary and regrettable war.[24] Perhaps the most revealing overall portrait of Vietnamese feelings about the conflict comes in another novel, *The Sorrow of War*, by Vietnamese author Bao Ninh. After presenting a harrowing, thinly fictionalized description of his service in the North Vietnamese army during the height of the American war, Bao Ninh ends on a somber note suggesting the ambivalence with which Vietnamese look back over their past. "Each of us carried in his heart a separate war which in many ways was totally different, despite our common cause," he writes of his generation of North Vietnamese. "We had different memories of people we'd known and of the war itself, and we had different destinies in the post-war years."[25] In Vietnam, as in the United States, contestation among those with different experiences and outlooks will likely continue for a long time to come.

NOTES

INTRODUCTION

1. Jeffrey P. Kimball, *To Reason Why: The Debate about the Causes of U.S. Involvement in the Vietnam War* (New York: McGraw-Hill, 1990), 1–3.

CHAPTER 1

1. Max Frankel, "The Lessons of Vietnam," *New York Times*, July 6, 1971.
2. Duong Van Mai Elliott, *Sacred Willow: Four Generations in the Life of a Vietnamese Family* (New York: Oxford University Press, 1999), 82.
3. William J. Duiker, *The Communist Road to Power in Vietnam*, 2nd ed. (Boulder, Colo.: Westview, 1996), 9.
4. Quoted in James W. Trullinger, *Village at War: An Account of Conflict in Vietnam* (Stanford, Calif.: Stanford University Press, 1980), 18.
5. Quoted in Ngo Vinh Long, *Before the Revolution: The Vietnamese Peasants under the French* (New York: Columbia University Press, 1991), 112.
6. Quoted in William J. Duiker, *Ho Chi Minh: A Life* (New York: Hyperion, 2000), 37.
7. Ibid., 98–99.

8. Ho Chi Minh, *Selected Writings, 1920–1969* (Hanoi: Foreign Languages Publishing House, 1977), 46.
9. Ibid., 50.

CHAPTER 2

1. Ho Chi Minh, *Selected Writings, 1920–1969* (Hanoi: Foreign Languages Publishing House, 1977), 53.
2. Memorandum of conversation between Roosevelt and Stalin, November 28, 1943, in Department of Defense, *United States–Vietnam Relations, 1945–1967* (Washington, D.C.: U.S. Government Printing Office, 1971), vol. 7, 25.
3. Stein Tønnesson, "La paix imposée par la Chine: L'accord franco-vietnamien du 6 mars 1946," in Charles-Robert Ageron et al., eds., *Cahiers de l'institut d'histoire du temps présent*, no. 34 (June 1996): 35–56.
4. Ho Chi Minh, *Selected Writings*, 68.
5. Zhdanov speech, September 22, 1947, in Jussi Hanhimäki and Odd Arne Westad, *The Cold War: A History in Documents and Eyewitness Accounts* (New York: Oxford University Press, 2003), 52.
6. Qiang Zhai, *China and the Vietnam Wars, 1950–1975* (Chapel Hill: University of North Carolina Press, 2000), 20–26.
7. Quoted in Chen Jian, *Mao's China and the Cold War* (Chapel Hill: University of North Carolina Press, 2001), 121.
8. Quoted in James W. Trullinger, *Village at War: An Account of Conflict in Vietnam* (Stanford, Calif.: Stanford University Press, 1980), 59.
9. Tillman Durdin, "Fighter on a Mission," *New York Times Magazine*, February 18, 1951, 18.
10. William J. Duiker, *Sacred War: Nationalism and Revolution in a Divided Vietnam* (New York: McGraw-Hill, 1995), 86.
11. Ibid., 79.
12. Joint Chiefs of Staff to Secretary of Defense, August 28, 1953, in Gareth Porter, *Vietnam: The Definitive Documentation of*

Human Decisions (Stanfordville, N.Y.: Coleman Enterprises, 1979), vol. 1, 463.

13. Karen Gottschang Turner with Phan Thanh Hao, *Even the Women Must Fight: Memories of War from North Vietnam* (New York: John Wiley and Sons, 1998), 31–32.

14. Quoted in George C. Herring and Richard Immerman, "Eisenhower, Dulles, and Dienbienphu: 'The Day We Didn't Go to War' Revisited," *Journal of American History* 71, no. 2 (September 1984): 353.

CHAPTER 3

1. Quoted in Lloyd C. Gardner, *Approaching Vietnam: From World War II through Dienbienphu* (New York: Norton, 1988), 265.

2. Quoted in Denis Warner, *The Last Confucian: Vietnam, South-East Asia, and the West*, revised ed. (Sydney: Angus and Robertson, 1964), 93.

3. Eisenhower news conference transcript, April 7, 1954, in *Public Papers of the Presidents of the United States: Dwight D. Eisenhower, 1954* (Washington, D.C.: U.S. Government Printing Office, 1960), 383.

4. Dulles to Undersecretary of State Walter Bedell Smith, May 12, 1954, in Department of Defense, *United States-Vietnam Relations, 1945–1967* (Washington, D.C.: U.S. Government Printing Office, 1971), vol. 9, 458.

5. Chen Jian, "China and the Indochina Settlement at the Geneva Conference of 1954," in *The Vietnam War: Colonial Conflict and Cold War Crisis*, ed. Mark Atwood Lawrence and Fredrik Logevall (Cambridge, Mass.: Harvard University Press, 2007), 253–259.

6. Geneva Accords, July 20, 1954, in Gareth Porter, ed., *Vietnam: The Definitive Documentation of Human Decisions* (Stanfordville, N.Y.: Coleman Enterprises, 1979), vol. 1, 642–653.

7. Statement by Bedell Smith, July 21, 1954, in *The Pentagon Papers: The Defense Department History of United States Decisionmaking on Vietnam*, Senator Gravel edition (Boston: Beacon, 1971), vol. 1, 571.

8. Quoted in George C. Herring, *America's Longest War: The United States and Vietnam, 1950–1975*, 4th ed. (New York: McGraw-Hill, 2002), 50.

9. Ibid., 51.

10. Quoted in David W. P. Elliott, *The Vietnamese War: Revolution and Social Change in the Mekong Delta, 1930–1975*, concise ed. (Armonk, N.Y.: M. E. Sharpe, 2007), 91.

11. Quoted in William J. Duiker, *Ho Chi Minh: A Life* (New York: Hyperion, 2000), 484.

12. Quoted in Seth Jacobs, *America's Miracle Man in Vietnam: Ngo Dinh Diem, Religion, Race, and U.S. Intervention in Southeast Asia* (Durham, N.C.: Duke University Press, 2004), 57.

13. Quoted in Marilyn B. Young, *The Vietnam Wars, 1945–1990* (New York: Harper, 1991), 58.

14. Eisenhower toast for Diem, May 8, 1957, in *Public Papers of the Presidents of the United States: Dwight D. Eisenhower, 1957* (Washington, D.C.: U.S. Government Printing Office, 1958), 335.

15. John Osborne, "The Tough Miracle Man of Vietnam," *Life*, May 13, 1957, 156.

16. William J. Lederer and Eugene Burdick, *The Ugly American* (New York: Norton, 1958).

17. Quoted in Elliott, *Vietnamese War*, 88.

18. Seth Jacobs, *Cold War Mandarin: Ngo Dinh Diem and the Origins of America's War in Vietnam, 1950–1963* (Lanham, Md.: Rowman and Littlefield, 2006), 96.

19. Mark Moyar, *Triumph Forsaken: The Vietnam War, 1954–1965* (New York: Cambridge University Press, 2006), 81.

20. Quoted in Jeffrey Race, *War Comes to Long An: Revolutionary Conflict in a Vietnamese Province* (Berkeley: University of California Press, 1972), 110.

21. Quoted in William J. Duiker, *Sacred War: Nationalism and Revolution in a Divided Vietnam* (New York: McGraw-Hill, 1995), 113.

22. William J. Duiker, *The Communist Road to Power in Vietnam*, 2nd ed. (Boulder, Colo.: Westview, 1996), 192.

23. Quoted in ibid., 200.

24. Moyar, *Triumph Forsaken*, 85.

25. Ibid., 91.

26. Quoted in Elliott, *Vietnamese War*, 104.

27. Durbrow to Secretary of State Christian A. Herter, September 16, 1960, in *The Pentagon Papers: The Defense Department History of United States Decisionmaking on Vietnam*, Senator Gravel edition (Boston: Beacon, 1971), vol. 2, 633.

CHAPTER 4

1. Memorandum for the National Security Council, "Program of Action to Prevent Communist Domination of South Viet Nam," May 9, 1961, box 330, National Security Files, John F. Kennedy Presidential Library, Boston, Massachusetts.

2. Kennedy inaugural address, *Public Papers of the Presidents of the United States: John F. Kennedy, 1961* (Washington, D.C.: U.S. Government Printing Office, 1962), 1.

3. Memorandum of conversation between Eisenhower and Kennedy, January 19, 1961, *The Pentagon Papers: The Defense Department History of United States Decisionmaking on Vietnam*, Senator Gravel edition (Boston: Beacon, 1971), vol. 2, 636.

4. William J. Duiker, *The Communist Road to Power in Vietnam*, 2nd ed. (Boulder, Colo.: Westview, 1996), 222–223.

5. Quoted in George McT. Kahin, *Intervention: How America Became Involved in Vietnam* (New York: Anchor, 1986), 474.

6. Mark Moyar, *Triumph Forsaken: The Vietnam War, 1954–1965* (New York: Cambridge University Press, 2006), 182.

7. Ibid., 185.

8. Quoted in Duiker, *Communist Road to Power*, 237.

9. "Manifesto of Vietnamese Buddhist Clergy and Faithful," May 10, 1963, *Foreign Relations of the United States, 1961–1963* (Washington, D.C.: U.S. Government Printing Office, 1991), vol. 3, 287.

10. Quoted in Seth Jacobs, *Cold War Mandarin: Ngo Dinh Diem and the Origins of America's War in Vietnam, 1950–1963* (Lanham, Md.: Rowman and Littlefield, 2006), 149.

11. Quoted in Duiker, *Communist Road to Power*, 237.

12. Quoted in Stanley Karnow, *Vietnam: A History* (New York: Penguin, 1983), 327.

13. Lien-Hang T. Nguyen, "The War Politburo: North Vietnam's Diplomatic and Political Road to the Tet Offensive," *Journal of Vietnamese Studies* 1, nos. 1–2 (2006), 16–18.

14. Bundy to Johnson, December 5, 1963, U.S. Department of State, *Foreign Relations of the United States, 1961–1963* (Washington, D.C.: U.S. Government Printing Office, 1996), vol. 8, 542.

15. Quoted in *The Pentagon Papers: The Defense Department History of United States Decisionmaking on Vietnam*, Senator Gravel edition (Boston: Beacon, 1971), vol. 2, 57.

16. Doris Kearns, *Lyndon Johnson and the American Dream* (New York: Harper and Row, 1976), 253.

17. Quoted in William Conrad Gibbons, *The U.S. Government and the Vietnam War: Executive and Legislative Roles and Relationships*, Part II, 1961–1964 (Princeton, N.J.: Princeton University Press, 1986), 233.

18. Telephone conversation, Johnson with Bundy, May 27, 1964, WH6405.10, no. 6, Lyndon Baines Johnson Presidential Library, Austin, Texas.

19. Gulf of Tonkin Resolution, August 7, 1964, in Gareth Porter, *Vietnam: The Definitive Documentation of Human Decisions* (Stanfordville, N.Y.: Coleman Enterprises, 1979), vol. 2, 307.

20. Johnson speech, October 12, 1964, in *Public Papers of the Presidents: Lyndon B. Johnson, 1963–64* (Washington, D.C.: U.S. Government Printing Office, 1965), vol. 2, 1391.

21. Bundy to Johnson, January 27, 1965, U.S. Department of State, *Foreign Relations of the United States, 1964–1968* (Washington, D.C.: U.S. Government Printing Office, 1996), vol. 2, 95–97.

22. Lyndon Baines Johnson, *The Vantage Point: Perspectives on the Presidency, 1963–1969* (New York: Holt, Rinehart, and Winston, 1971), 125.

CHAPTER 5

1. Quoted in Robert Mann, *A Grand Delusion: America's Descent into Vietnam* (New York: Basic Books, 2001), 420.
2. Le Duan speech to party conference, July 6–8, 1965, in Gareth Porter, *Vietnam: The Definitive Documentation of Human Decisions* (Stanfordville, N.Y.: Coleman Enterprises, 1979), vol. 2, 383.
3. Johnson speech, April 7, 1965, in *Public Papers of the Presidents of the United States: Lyndon B. Johnson, 1965* (Washington, D.C.: U.S. Government Printing Office, 1966), vol. 1, 396–397.
4. Quoted in William J. Duiker, *The Communist Road to Power in Vietnam*, 2nd ed. (Boulder, Colo.: Westview, 1996), 265.
5. Ibid., 261.
6. Quoted in Qiang Zhai, *China and the Vietnam Wars, 1950–1975* (Chapel Hill: University of North Carolina Press, 2000), 133.
7. Quoted in Randall B. Woods, *LBJ: Architect of American Ambition* (New York: Free Press, 2006), 600.
8. Note of Johnson's meeting with advisers, July 21–22, 1965, in Michael H. Hunt, ed., *Crises in U.S. Foreign Policy: An International History Reader* (New Haven, Conn.: Yale University Press, 1996), 354.
9. Quoted in Christian G. Appy, *Patriots: The Vietnam War Remembered from All Sides* (New York: Viking, 2003), 191.
10. George Donelson Moss, *Vietnam: An American Ordeal*, 5th ed. (Upper Saddle River, N.J.: Prentice Hall, 2006), 263.
11. Quoted in Mann, *Grand Delusion*, 416.
12. Mark Clodfelter, *The Limits of Air Power: The American Bombing of North Vietnam* (New York: Free Press, 1989), 134–135.
13. Quoted in David Chanoff and Doan Van Toai, eds., *"Vietnam": A Portrait of Its People at War* (London: I. B. Tauris, 2001), 63.

14. Clodfelter, *Limits of Air Power*, 134–135.
15. Ibid., 134.
16. Jon M. Van Dyke, *North Vietnam's Strategy for Survival* (Palo Alto, Calif.: Pacific Books, 1972), 67.
17. William J. Duiker, *Sacred War: Nationalism and Revolution in a Divided Vietnam* (New York: McGraw-Hill, 1995), 200.
18. Quoted in Shaun Malarney, "The Realities and Consequences of War in a Northern Vietnamese Commune," in *A Companion to the Vietnam War*, ed. Marilyn B. Young and Robert Buzzanco (Malden, Mass.: Blackwell, 2002), 71.
19. Duiker, *Sacred War*, 201.
20. Quoted in David W. P. Elliott, *The Vietnamese War: Revolution and Social Change in the Mekong Delta, 1930–1975*, concise ed. (Armonk, N.Y.: M. E. Sharpe, 2007), 299.
21. Jeffrey Race, *War Comes to Long An: A Revolutionary Conflict in a Vietnamese Province* (Berkeley: University of California Press, 1972), 219.
22. Quoted in Duiker, *Communist Road to Power*, 274.
23. Quoted in Christian Appy, *Working Class War: American Combat Soldiers and Vietnam* (Chapel Hill: University of North Carolina Press, 1993), 163–164.
24. Quoted in Al Santoli, *Everything We Had: An Oral History of the Vietnam War by Thirty-Three American Soldiers Who Fought It* (New York: Ballantine, 1981), 59.
25. James W. Trullinger, *Village at War: An Account of Conflict in Vietnam* (Stanford, Calif.: Stanford University Press, 1980), 143.
26. Tom Wicker, "Johnson-Ky Talks Begin with Accord on Reforms as a Key to Winning War," *New York Times*, February 8, 1966.
27. George C. Herring, *America's Longest War: The United States and Vietnam, 1950–1975*, 4th ed. (New York: McGraw-Hill, 2002), 201.
28. Melvin Small, *Antiwarriors: The Vietnam War and the Battle for America's Hearts and Minds* (Wilmington, Del.: Scholarly Resources, 2002), 55.
29. Ibid., 76.

CHAPTER 6

1. Quoted in Christian G. Appy, *Patriots: The Vietnam War Remembered from All Sides* (New York: Viking, 2003), 285.
2. Quoted in David F. Schmitz, *The Tet Offensive: Politics, War, and Public Opinion* (Lanham, Md.: Rowman and Littlefield, 2005), 112.
3. Quoted in ibid., 55–56.
4. Marilyn B. Young, *The Vietnam Wars, 1945–1990* (New York: Harper, 1991), 214.
5. Robert Mann, *A Grand Delusion: America's Descent into Vietnam* (New York: Basic Books, 2001), 567.
6. Quoted in Robert S. McNamara, *In Retrospect: The Tragedy and Lessons of Vietnam* (New York: Times Books, 1995), 269.
7. Quoted in Don Oberdorfer, *Tet! The Turning Point in the Vietnam War*, new ed. (Baltimore: Johns Hopkins University Press, 2001), 105.
8. Lien-Hang T. Nguyen, "The War Politburo: North Vietnam's Diplomatic and Political Road to the Tet Offensive," *Journal of Vietnamese Studies* 1, nos. 1–2 (2006): 4–58.
9. Province Party Standing Committee to local party committees, November 1, 1967, in Michael H. Hunt, ed., *Crises in U.S. Foreign Policy: An International History Reader* (New Haven, Conn.: Yale University Press, 1996), 362.
10. Quoted in Ang Cheng Guan, *The Vietnam War from the Other Side: The Vietnamese Communists' Perspective* (London: Routledge Curzon, 2002), 127.
11. Quoted in Schmitz, *Tet Offensive*, 84.
12. Quoted in Randall B. Woods, *LBJ: Architect of American Ambition* (New York: Free Press, 2006), 825.
13. Quoted in Schmitz, *Tet Offensive*, 109.
14. John W. Finney, "Rusk Tells Panel of 'A to Z' Review of Vietnam War," *New York Times*, March 12, 1968.
15. Schmitz, *Tet Offensive*, 135.

16. Johnson speech, March 31, 1968, in *Public Papers of the Presidents of the United States: Lyndon B. Johnson, 1968–1969* (Washington, D.C.: U.S. Government Printing Office, 1970), vol. 1, 469–476.

17. Ang Cheng Guan, *Vietnam War*, 131–132.

18. Quoted in William J. Duiker, *Sacred War: Nationalism and Revolution in a Divided Vietnam* (New York: McGraw-Hill, 1995), 216.

19. Quoted in Ronald Spector, *After Tet: The Bloodiest Year in Vietnam* (New York: Vintage, 1993), 82.

20. Melvin Small, *Antiwarriors: The Vietnam War and the Battle for America's Hearts and Minds* (Wilmington, Del.: Scholarly Resources, 2002), 97–99.

21. Lien-Hang T. Nguyen, "Tét Mâu Thân: Myths and Mysteries, 1967–1968," chapter in " 'Between the Storms': North Vietnam's Strategy during the Second Indochina War, 1955–1973" (Ph.D. diss., Yale University, 2008), 38.

Chapter 7

1. Robert B. Semple Jr., "Nixon Withholds His Peace Ideas," *New York Times*, March 11, 1968.

2. Quoted in H. R. Haldeman with Joseph DiMona, *The Ends of Power* (New York: Times Books, 1978), 81.

3. Kissinger to Nixon, September 18, 1971, in Jeffrey Kimball, *The Vietnam War Files: Uncovering the Secret History of Nixon-Era Strategy* (Lawrence: University Press of Kansas, 2004), 46.

4. Quoted in Haldeman, *Ends of Power*, 82.

5. Central Office for South Vietnam (COSVN) Resolution Number 9, July 1969, in Gareth Porter, ed., *Vietnam: A History in Documents* (New York: New American Library, 1981), 383.

6. Dang Thuy Tram, *Last Night I Dreamed of Peace*, trans. Andrew X. Pham (New York: Harmony Books, 2007), 125.

7. Military History Institute of Vietnam, *Victory in Vietnam: The Official History of the People's Army of Vietnam, 1954–1975*, trans. Merle Pribbenow (Lawrence: University Press of Kansas, 2002), 243.

8. Memorandum of conversation, Li Xiannian and Le Duc Tho, in Odd Arne Westad et al., eds., "77 Conversations between Chinese and Foreign Leaders on the Wars in Indochina, 1964–1977," Working Paper No. 22, Cold War International History Project, Woodrow Wilson International Center for Scholars, Washington, D.C., May 1998, 160.

9. Melvin Small, *Antiwarriors: The Vietnam War and the Battle for America's Hearts and Minds* (Wilmington, Del.: Scholarly Resources, 2002), 112.

10. Agnew speech, October 30, 1969, in *Collected Speeches of Spiro Agnew* (New York: Audubon, 1971), 73.

11. Nixon speech, November 3, 1969, in *Public Papers of the Presidents of the United States, Richard Nixon, 1969* (Washington, D.C.: U.S. Government Printing Office, 1971), 909.

12. George C. Herring, *America's Longest War: The United States and Vietnam, 1950–1975*, 4th ed. (New York: McGraw-Hill, 2002), 284.

13. Quoted in Roger Morris, *Uncertain Greatness: Henry Kissinger and American Foreign Policy* (New York: Harper and Row, 1977), 164.

14. Quoted in Herring, *America's Longest War*, 290

15. Quoted in Small, *Antiwarriors*, 123.

16. Quoted in Robert Dallek, *Nixon and Kissinger: Partners in Power* (New York: HarperCollins, 2007), 200–201.

17. David W. P. Elliott, *The Vietnamese War: Revolution and Social Change in the Mekong Delta, 1930–1975*, concise ed. (Armonk, N.Y.: M. E. Sharpe, 2007), 372.

18. Quoted in Jeffrey Kimball, *Nixon's Vietnam War* (Lawrence: University Press of Kansas, 1998), 247.

19. Kerry statement before Senate Foreign Relations Committee, April 22, 1971, in Robert J. McMahon, ed., *Major Problems in the History of the Vietnam War*, 2nd ed. (Lexington, Mass.: D.C. Heath, 1995), 486.

20. Quoted in Christian G. Appy, *Working Class War: American Combat Soldiers and Vietnam* (Chapel Hill: University of North Carolina Press, 1993), 247.

21. Louis Harris, "Tide of Public Opinion Turns Decisively against the War," *Washington Post*, May 3, 1971, A14.

22. Kissinger briefing book, July 1971, in Kimball, *Vietnam War Files*, 187.

23. Resolution of the Twentieth Plenum of the Vietnamese Workers Party Central Committee, January 27–February 11, 1972, in Van Kien Dang [Party Records], comp. Dang Cong San [Communist Party] (Hanoi: Chinh Tri Quoc Gia, 2004), vol. 33, 14–138.

24. Quoted in Dallek, *Nixon and Kissinger*, 372.

25. Quoted in Seymour M. Hersh, *The Price of Power: Kissinger in the Nixon White House* (New York: Summit Books, 1983), 506.

26. Quoted in Elliott, *Vietnamese War*, 403.

27. Quoted in Jussi Hanhimäki, *The Flawed Architect: Henry Kissinger and American Foreign Policy* (New York: Oxford University Press, 2004), 242.

28. Bernard Gwertzman, "Kissinger Asserts That 'Peace Is at Hand,' " *New York Times*, October 27, 1972.

29. Quoted in Hanhimäki, *Flawed Architect*, 253.

30. Quoted in William Bundy, *A Tangled Web: The Making of Foreign Policy in the Nixon Presidency* (New York: Hill and Wang, 1999), 362.

31. Bernard Gwertzman, "Vietnam Accord Is Reached," *New York Times*, January 24, 1973.

Chapter 8

1. Joseph B. Treaster, "Among the Last GI's: Joy, Anger, and Disbelief," *New York Times*, January 25, 1973.

2. William J. Duiker, *The Communist Road to Power in Vietnam*, 2nd ed. (Boulder, Colo.: Westview, 1996), 333.

3. Robert D. Schulzinger, *A Time for War: The United States and Vietnam, 1941–1975* (New York: Oxford University Press, 1997), 311.

4. James W. Trullinger, *Village at War: An Account of Conflict in Vietnam* (Stanford, Calif.: Stanford University Press, 1980), 193.

5. David W. P. Elliott, *The Vietnamese War: Revolution and Social Change in the Mekong Delta, 1930–1975*, concise ed. (Armonk, N.Y.: M. E. Sharpe, 2007), 424.

6. Richard L. Madden, "Ford Says Indochina War Is Finished for America," *New York Times*, April 24, 1975.

7. Malcolm W. Browne, "Thieu Resigns; Calls U.S. Untrustworthy," *New York Times*, April 22, 1975.

8. Trullinger, *Village at War*, 209.

9. For a glimpse of the debate, see Jacqueline Desbarats, "Repression in the Socialist Republic of Vietnam: Executions and Population Relocation," in *The Vietnam Debate: A Fresh Look at the Arguments*, ed. John Norton Moore (Lanham, Md.: University Press of America, 1990), 193–201.

10. W. Courtland Robinson, *Terms of Refuge: The Indochinese Exodus and the International Response* (New York: Zed Books, 1998), 27.

11. Jane Hamilton-Merritt, *Tragic Mountains: The Hmong, the Americans, and the Secret Wars for Laos, 1942–1992* (Bloomington: University of Indiana Press, 1993).

12. Richard L. Madden, "President Vows Nation Will Keep Pledges Abroad," *New York Times*, May 4, 1975.

13. Carter speech, May 22, 1977, in *Public Papers of the Presidents, James E. Carter, 1977* (Washington, D.C.: U.S. Government Printing Office, 1978), vol. 1, 956–957.

14. Quoted in James T. Patterson, *Restless Giant: The United States from Watergate to Bush v. Gore* (New York: Oxford University Press, 2005), 73.

15. Fred Turner, *Echoes of Combat: The Vietnam War in American Memory* (New York: Anchor Books, 1996), 61.

16. Howell Raines, "Reagan Calls Arms Race Essential to Void a 'Surrender' or 'Defeat,'" *New York Times*, August 19, 1980.

17. Robert D. Schulzinger, *A Time for Peace: The Legacy of the Vietnam War* (New York: Oxford University Press, 2006), 191.

18. Edwin McDowell, "Publishing: Vietnam Remembered," *New York Times*, December 2, 1983.

19. *First Blood,* directed by Ted Kotcheff (1982; DVD, Vancouver: Lion's Gate, 2004).

20. James S. Olson and Randy Roberts, *Where the Domino Fell: America and Vietnam, 1945–2004,* 4th ed. (Maplecrest, N.Y.: Brandywine Press, 2004), 277.

21. Bennett Roth, "U.S. Viewing Vietnam as a Country, Not a War," *Houston Chronicle,* November 17, 2000.

22. George C. Herring, "America and Vietnam: The Unending War," *Foreign Affairs* 70, no. 5 (Winter 1991–1992).

23. United Nations Development Program, *Human Development Report, 2006* (New York: Palgrave Macmillan, 2006), 285.

24. Duong Thu Huong, *Paradise of the Blind* (New York: Harper, 1993; originally published in Vietnamese, 1989).

25. Bao Ninh, *The Sorrow of War* (London: Secker and Warburg, 1993; originally published in Vietnamese, 1991), 216.

FURTHER READING

The literature on the Vietnam War is extraordinarily vast. This brief guide, intended as a mere starting point for further reading, highlights some of the most insightful and accessible recent books, along with a few older titles that remain especially notable. It omits highly specialized studies, although some of these are mentioned in the endnotes to this book.

Outstanding surveys of the Vietnam War emphasizing U.S. policymaking include George C. Herring, *America's Longest War;* Robert J. McMahon, *The Limits of Empire;* Robert D. Schulzinger, *A Time for War;* and Marilyn B. Young, *The Vietnam Wars.* For overviews of the Viet Minh and North Vietnamese side of the war, the most authoritative books are William J. Duiker's two surveys, *Sacred War* and *The Communist Road to Power in Vietnam,* and Cheng Guan Ang's *The Vietnam War from the Other Side.*

The effects of French colonialism and the development of Vietnamese nationalism are brilliantly explored in David Marr, *Vietnamese Tradition on Trial;* Hyunh Kim Khanh, *Vietnamese Communism;* Sophie Quinn-Judge, *Ho Chi Minh: The Missing Years;* and William J. Duiker, *Ho Chi Minh: A Life.* On the end of the Second World War and the August Revolution, David Marr's *1945* offers a remarkable blow-by-blow account of events in Vietnam.

For the Franco–Viet Minh War and the emergence of conflict in Vietnam as a Cold War crisis, see Mark Philip Bradley, *Imagining*

Vietnam and America; Lloyd C. Gardner, *Approaching Vietnam;* Mark Atwood Lawrence, *Assuming the Burden;* and Andrew Rotter, *The Path to Vietnam.* The most engaging account of the Battle of Dien Bien Phu is Bernard Fall's 1966 classic *Hell in a Very Small Place.* Newly available documents in China and Russia have revolutionized the study of the Geneva Conference. The most revealing books on this issue—and on policymaking by the communist powers throughout the Vietnam conflict—are Chen Jian, *Mao's China and the Cold War;* Qiang Zhai, *China and the Vietnam Wars;* and Ilya Gaiduk's two studies of Soviet policymaking, *The Soviet Union and the Vietnam War* and *Confronting Vietnam.*

Important studies of Ngo Dinh Diem and the "nation-building" years include David L. Anderson, *Trapped by Success;* Philip E. Catton, *Diem's Final Failure;* Seth Jacobs, *America's Miracle Man in Vietnam;* and Kathryn Statler, *Replacing France,* although two novels from the 1950s—*The Quiet American* by Graham Greene and *The Ugly American* by William J. Lederer and Eugene Burdick—may be the best starting points for understanding the period. On the escalation of the U.S. commitment during the Kennedy and Johnson administrations, see Fredrik Logevall, *Choosing War;* David G. Kaiser, *American Tragedy;* and Andrew Preston, *The War Council.* Also valuable are David Halberstam's classic *The Best and the Brightest* and Robert McNamara's controversial memoir, *In Retrospect.*

The U.S. bombing campaign is well covered in Mark Clodfelter's *The Limits of Air Power,* while numerous insightful studies explore the ground war. Christian G. Appy's *Working Class War* and Frank F. Krepinovich Jr.'s *The Army in Vietnam* examine the performance of American ground forces. Memoirs and oral histories are also extremely revealing. See, for example, Christian G. Appy, *Patriots;* Philip Caputo, *A Rumor of War;* Al Santoli, *Everything We Had;* Wallace Terry, *Bloods;* and Linda Van Devanter, *Home before Morning.*

For compelling analysis of the experiences of Vietnamese soldiers and civilians, see Jeffrey Race, *War Comes to Long An;* James W. Trullinger, *Village at War;* Karen Gottschang Turner, *Even the Women Must*

Fight; and especially David W. P. Elliott's monumental *The Vietnamese War.* Robert K. Brigham's *ARVN* provides insight into the performance of the South Vietnamese army, and Brigham's *Guerrilla Diplomacy* examines the complex relationship between Hanoi and the National Liberation Front. Duong Van Mai Elliott's memoir, *The Sacred Willow,* offers a rich portrait of life in Vietnam before and during the American war. For reminiscences by Vietnamese soldiers, diplomats, and civilians, see David Chanoff and Doan Van Toai's *"Vietnam"* and Appy's *Patriots.* Vietnamese attempts to understand the war's significance within their national history are examined by Patricia M. Pelley in *Postcolonial Vietnam.* Powerful novels by Vietnamese authors include Bao Ninh's *The Sorrow of War* and Duong Thu Huong's *Paradise of the Blind.*

The most engaging account of the Tet Offensive remains Don Oberdorfer's classic *Tet!* although David F. Schmitz's *The Tet Offensive* provides more up-to-date analysis of decision making in the United States. Notable studies of American policy during the Nixon years include Larry Berman, *No Peace, No Honor;* Jussi Hanhimäki, *The Flawed Architect;* Jeffrey Kimball, *Nixon's Vietnam War;* and Lewis Sorley, *A Better War.* On the Vietnamese side of the Paris negotiations, see Pierre Asselin's *A Bitter Peace.* A riveting account of the war in Vietnam following the peace agreement is Arnold R. Isaacs, *Without Honor.*

On American domestic politics and the antiwar movement, see Maurice Isserman and Michael Kazin, *America Divided;* David Maraniss, *They Marched into Sunlight;* Tom Wells, *The War Within;* and two books by Melvin Small, *Johnson, Nixon, and the Doves* and *Antiwarriors.* The most vivid reading on the antiwar movement, however, comes from memoirists. See, for example, James Carroll's *American Requiem* and David Harris's *Dreams Die Hard.*

Ben Kiernan's *The Pol Pot Regime* provides the best overview of the Khmer Rouge, and Jane Hamilton-Merritt's *Tragic Mountains* examines the war in Laos and the fate of the Hmong. On the international impact of the U.S. defeat, Odd Arne Westad's *The Global Cold War* is

204 • FURTHER READING

without peer. Valuable studies of the war's effects on American politics and culture include Tom Engelhardt, *The End of Victory Culture;* H. Bruce Franklin, *MIA, or Mythmaking in America;* Robert D. Schulzinger, *A Time for Peace;* and Fred Turner, *Echoes of Combat.* On parallels between the wars in Vietnam and Iraq, see Robert K. Brigham's *Is Iraq Another Vietnam?*

INDEX

Page numbers in bold indicate illustrations.